CYBER

AN ERA OF CRIME & LAWS

AKASH RAMAKANT SHARMA

AF658040

BlueRose ONE .com
Stories Matter
NewDelhi • London

Justice Ravi Malimath
CHIEF JUSTICE

191, South Civil Lines,
JABALPUR - 482 001
Phone : 0761-2678855 (R)
: 0761-2626746 (R)
: 0761-2626443 (O)
Fax : 0761-2678833

20th June, 2022

FOREWORD

It gives me pleasure to know that Shri Akash Sharma, Advocate has written a book titled 'Cyber – An Era of Crime & Laws' and is proposing to publish the same.

Study of Cyber laws in the Indian perspective is important, because of the prime reason that, in today's techno-savvy environment, the world is becoming more and more digitally sophisticated and so are the crimes. As the number of internet users is on the rise, the need for cyber laws is all the more imminent.

I extend my congratulations to Shri Akash Sharma for his efforts in bringing out this book. I hope that this book will be useful to the Judges, Judicial Officers, Lawyers and all other stakeholders.

(Justice Ravi Malimath)

Justice Vivek Rusia
JUDGE
High Court of Madhya Pradesh

Bungalow No.A-1, Pili Kothi
Judges' Enclave, M.G. Road,
Indore (M.P.) - 452 001
Phone :0731-2430022 (R)
0731-2520068 (O)
Mobile : 7587593002
E-mail : vivekrusia@yahoo.com

25.02.2022

Dear Akash Sharma Advocate,

In the rising era of Information Technology and its varied applications in today's world, it is great to know that you have written a book "Cyber-A New Era of Crime & Laws" that acknowledges the laws and crimes pertaining to cyberspace. Considering the vastness of the aspects of cybercrimes and the magnitude of the laws available to deal with them, a literary work that elucidates the concepts through explanations and illustrations is the need of the hour.

This book will serve as a guide for the legal fraternity as well the general public alike who wish to equip themselves with the knowledge of Cyber Crime, Cyber Law and the rights of the public. A fair understanding of such concepts through this book can also help save people from instances of cybercrime.

I appreciate your work and wish you a bright future ahead.

Best wishes,

Justice Vivek Rusia

VIVEK RUSIA
Administrative Judge
High Court of M.P.
Bench at Indore

प्रशान्त सिंह
महाधिवक्ता
मध्यप्रदेश शासन

अर्द्ध. शास. पत्र क्र.
कार्यालय महाधिवक्ता मध्यप्रदेश
जबलपुर (म.प्र.) पिन - 482007
फोन : (O) 0761- 2678740, 2678185
फैक्स : (O) 0761-2621216
दिनांक

25/4/2022

Dear Advocate Akash R Sharma,

In the current scenario of the Information Technology it's a good step from you by writing a book "Cyber- A New Era of Crime & Laws" on Cyberworld. As the world is moving towards the Information Technology by various means, it is also necessary to have the acknowledgments about the modern ways of crimes and also needs to get safer from them. Your book pertaining to Cyber World is a good initiative by gathering a good source of information in terms of vast aspects of the Cyber Crimes and laws for the people's awareness and acknowledgment.

The book is very nice for the legal entities as well as the public in terms of understanding of the Cyber Crime, Cyber Law and the Rights of the Public and you have done apreciable effort to fill up the gap of availability of understandable literature in this field.

I appreciate your's work and wishes for your bright future.

PRASHANT SINGH

निवास : "आराधना", 297, राईट टाउन, जबलपुर (म.प्र.)
मोबाइल : 9425804707 | ई-मेल : advocategeneralmp@gmail.com, advgenjab@mp.gov.in
advprashantsinghassociates@gmail.com

Dr. VARUN KAPOOR
I.P.S.
Addl. Director General of Police

Rustamji Armed Police Training College,
VIP Road, Indore - 452005
Mobile : 98260-17614
E-mail : varunkapoor170@gmail.com

Dated: 14th April 2022

Dear Akash,

I came to know that you are coming out with a book entitled "**Cyber- A New Era of Crime & Laws**". In today's world information and the technologies associated with it are of paramount importance. Along with the positive use of these resources there is also a growing trend of its misuse. As a result Cyber crimes as well as Cyber insecurities are increasing rapidly and are posing a grave threat to the common citizens peace and tranquillity.

The best and only way to ensure security of citizens in the cyber space is by enhancing their awareness. And your effort in this direction are appreciable as you are writing a book in this sphere which will contribute immensely in raising peoples awareness regarding the types of cyber offences and ways and means of protection against them. The information that you will impart regarding IT Act will add value to the content.

I wish you all the best in this as well as all future endeavours that you may undertake.

Best Wishes

(Varun Kapoor, IPS)

To,
Mr. Akash R Sharma
Advocate

Preface

Today, technology is becoming the means of life which includes Education, Business, Transactions, Entertainment, Connections, modes of expression, etc. Without acknowledging that any sort of act has a different consequence as the use of technology is rising day by day the rate of crime is also increasing day by day, because people lack knowledge about the use of technology and its consequences struck in the trap of the cybercriminals.

This Book describes Cyber Crime, security measures to deal with it and the Laws and Rights available to citizens in the simple and easy language.

This Book has been written after collecting vast information from every aspect and I had tried to provide most of the knowledge about Cyber and its Laws.

I tried to relate this book with the daily happenings and covered phenomena which happens in the daily life routine of an ordinary person to understand the book in a relatable style.

I have tried to define every legal term in the Law which can help people understand, if anything unlawful has happened to them as well as providing measures to safeguard them.

I hope you will like my work and understand about cyber crimes, laws and it's provisions.

Akash Ramakant Sharma

Contents

Chapter one

Introduction

Crime is a legal wrong the remedy for which is punishment of the offender at the instance of the state. It is a legal concept having the sanction of the law. Crime is a social and economic phenomenon found in the oldest human society. Crime is defined as an act, which subjects the doer to legal punishment or any offence against morality, social order or any unjust or shameful act, and the term "offence" is defined in the Code of Criminal Procedure to mean "an act or omission made punishable by any law for the time being in force." It is a social and economical phenomenon and is as old as the human society.

Crime or an offence is a legal wrong that can be followed by criminal proceedings which may result in punishment. Moreover, the moral sentiments and values of a society or a country are flexible, changing from time to time and place to place. Committing *'Sati'* was not a crime in India until it was declared by legislation. Polygamy was allowed in India up to 1955 and it was not a crime but by the Hindu Marriage Act, 1955, it's a crime.

Thus, what was a virtue yesterday may become a crime tomorrow and *vice versa*. Consequently, the content of a crime is volatile and fluctuates from time to time in the same country at the same time.

Today's is an era of the internet and information technology in which each and every person in this world has acknowledgment of the internet which can be availed on various devices For example, smart phones, tablets, computers, etc. and there are uncountable users of internet using that either by the cellular network or Wi-Fi.

Internet is a massive worldwide network of computers connected with the main objective of sharing and transmitting information and there are many people in the world who are using the Internet for various means whether it is for entertainment, business, education, banking, socializing, etc. that creates a world of people connected with each other through the internet and this internet connectivity commonly known as "**CYBER WORLD**" and in the cyber world where these activities are to be done is known as **"CYBER SPACE".**

Information Technology and Information Services have a massive effect on the country's economy, trade, and commerce. The Securities and Exchange Board of India has allowed trading on the Internet. The Stock Exchange in India is carrying out different kinds of transactions and information exchange of their networks. The Reserve Bank of India has introduced the electronic payment system.

As the use of the internet or information technology has increased there are so many people who are taking benefit of it and leads a part in developing the country whereas there are so many people's also who are indulging in using it for their Criminal activities and increase the crime backhandedly by various of means like **Hacking, phishing, fraud, pornography (for detail see Chapter Seven)** etc. In the recent scenario it has been seen that as the users of the internet have been added to this Cyber World there is a tremendous increment in the Cyber Crime itself of both the doers and the victims and it is boosting day by day due to lacuna in services lack in Cyber Security and less knowledge as well as awareness regarding Cyber Crimes in the public.

There have been concerns from Intelligence and Law Enforcement Agencies and others about Computer Crime, Computer misuse, data protection, security standards, intellectual property rights, privacy etc.

Chapter Two

Cyber Crime

"Criminal activities carried out by means of computers or the Internet." –Oxford Dictionary

The term "cyber" is derived from the term "cybernetics" which means the science of communication and control over machine and man. Cyberspace is the new horizon which is controlled by machines for information and communication between human beings across the world. Therefore, crimes committed in cyberspace relating to machines or devices or cyber technology-related crimes are to be treated as cyber crimes.

cyber crime is outlined as crimes committed on the internet and mistreatment of the PC as either a tool or a targeted victim. It is tough to classify crimes generally into distinct teams as several crimes evolve day after day.

Cyber is a prefix used in a growing number of terms to describe new things that are being made possible by the spread of computers and devices. Anything related to the internet also falls under the cyber category.

Technological advancement specifically in the fields of communication and information opens new ventures for human beings including criminals. Criminal-minded people misused the said revolution for the enhancement of their criminal activities.

cyber crime is the most recent type of crime which affects many people. This is the biggest challenge for police, prosecutors, and lawmakers.

cyber crimes can be defined as: "Offences that are committed against individuals or groups of individuals with a criminal motive to intentionally harm the reputation of the victim or cause physical or mental harm, or loss, to the victim directly or indirectly, using modern telecommunication networks such as the Internet (networks including chat rooms, emails, notice boards, and groups) and mobile phones (Bluetooth/SMS/MMS)". cyber crime may threaten a person or a nation's security and financial health. Issues surrounding these types of crimes have become high-profile, particularly those regarding hacking, copyright infringement, unwarranted mass-surveillance, sextortion, child pornography, and child grooming.

Difference Between Traditional and Cyber Crime

Figure 1: Comparison between Traditional Criminal Techniques and Cybercrime

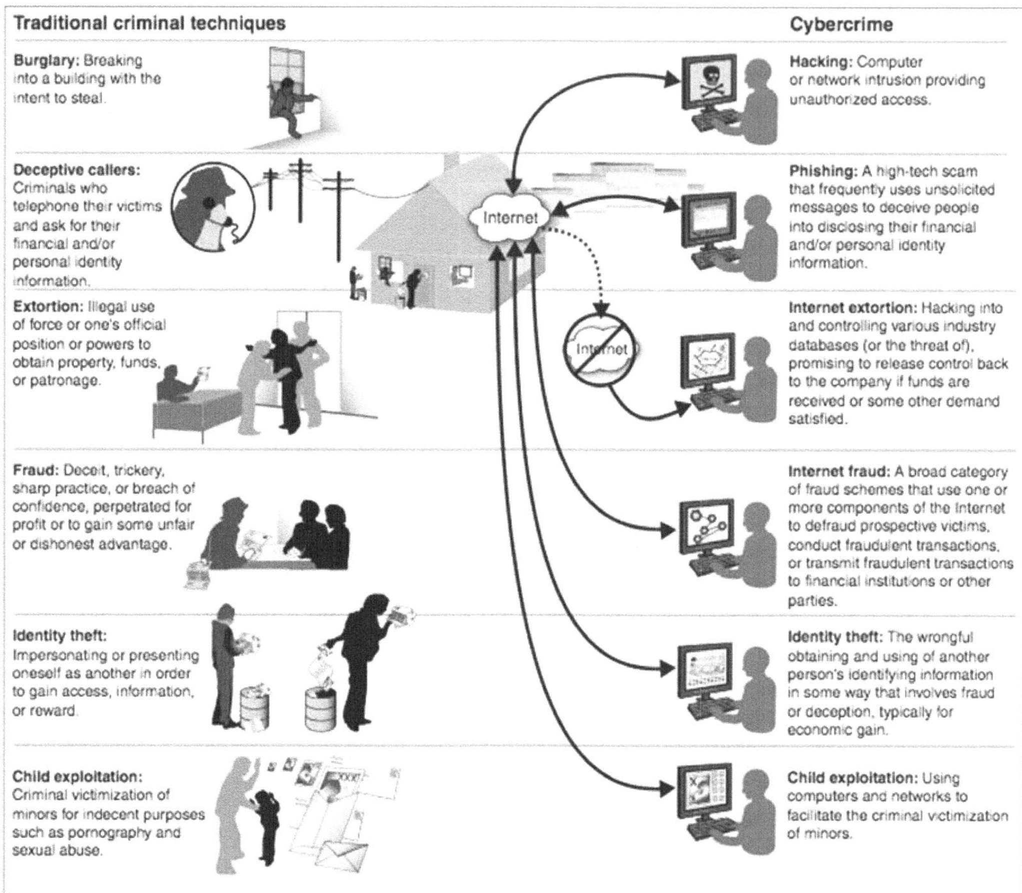

Source: GAO

Chapter Three

Cyber Criminals

Cyber criminal is a person who commits an illegal act with a guilty intention or commits a crime in context to cyber crime. Cyber criminal can be motivated criminals, organised hackers, , discontented employees, cyber terrorists etc. Cyber crime can include everything from non-delivery of goods or services and computer intrusions (hacking) to intellectual property rights abuses, economic espionage (theft of trade secrets), online extortion, international money laundering, identity theft, and a growing list of other Internet-facilitated offenses.

Cyber criminals are majorly of three categories:-

i). Idealists

Cyber Criminals who come under this category are committing or have committed the crime to achieve a limelight to be famous in the public as not being traced after being commitment of crime. They are generally involved in crimes like hacking, introducing viruses etc.

ii). Greedy

Cyber criminals come under this category are different from idealists as they commit the crime for the fulfillment of their need to earn money through the internet. The offence committed by them is procures heavy damages. These offences are like financial fraud, cyber terrorism etc.

iii). Revenge

Cyber criminals under this category are very different from above as this kind of criminals have neither intention to get fame nor earning of money or else. These kinds of criminals only have the intention to do bad to a particular person or company either to defame or to make a loss to them by abusing or disclosing their information or activity. These criminals includes employee terrorists etc.

Cyber criminals try to use the computers in three broad ways:-

i). Firstly, they use the computer as their target for attacking other people's computers to fulfil their malicious activities like spreading viruses, data theft, identity theft, etc.,

ii). Secondly, they use the computer as their weapon to carry out conventional crimes like spam, fraud, illegal gambling, etc., and iii). Thirdly, they use the computer as their accessory to save stolen or illegal data.

Unlike traditional offenders, cyber criminals are hi-tech knowledgeable person who invade the rights of computer users by unauthorized access to their computer system or computer network. Usually, they indulge in techno-vandalism by unauthorized access which causes damage to files and programs of the computer user. They are engaging in this type of activity not necessarily for monetary gain but also may be prompted by an adventure or maybe to harass the victim.

Chapter Four

Reasons for Cyber Crime

Hart in his work "The Concept of Law" has said 'human beings are vulnerable so the rule of law is required to protect them'. Applying this to cyberspace we may say that computers are vulnerable so the rule of law is required to protect and safeguard them against cyber crime.

The reasons for the vulnerability of computers may be said to be:

i). Huge data Storage

Today from a common man to a businessman, from a personal office to a government office, personal letters to military secrets everything is in a computer or device because the computer has a unique characteristic of storing data in a very small space. A small pen drive or chip can store billions of pages, records, videos various kinds of data, etc. This makes it a lot easier for people to steal data from any other storage and use it for their profit.

ii). Ease of Access

The one of major problems behind safeguarding a computer system from unauthorized access is that today everything is done on a computer or computer network and there are many possibilities of breach due to the complex technology and lack of security, lacuna in protective services in the computer systems and network. Hackers can steal access codes, retina images, advanced voice recorders, etc. that can fool biometric systems easily and bypass firewalls can be utilized to get past many security systems.

iii). Complex

The computers run on operating systems and these operating systems are programmed of millions of codes. The human mind is imperfect, so they can make mistakes at any stage. Cyber criminals take advantage of these gaps and get access to the system till the victim acknowledges about the unauthorised access, the criminal done his work and left that before his acknowledgment.

iv). Negligence

Negligence is one of the characteristics of human conduct and negligence is one of the biggest reasons for the increment in cyber crimes. Negligence can be securing passwords or frequently changing of password or using the same password everywhere, data, installation of unsecured software etc. So, there may be a possibility that in protecting the computer system we may make any negligence which provides a cyber-criminal the access and control over the computer system.

v). Loss of evidence

The crime that is being committed or has been committed never needs the physical presence and the server from which the crime used to be committed can be easily switched. The offender can easily hide his identity which saves him from identification and there are no territorial boundaries in cyber crime as well as data related to the crime can be easily destroyed. So, loss of evidence has become a very common & obvious problem which paralyzes the system behind the investigation of cyber-crime.

vi). Lack of Knowledge

In India, there are still so many people who are using the internet but still do not having any knowledge regarding the cyber crimes which is also one of the biggest reasons for increment of cyber crimes. Cyber criminals mostly attacks people who have no or little knowledge.

vii). Greed

In India, the most common type of cyber crime is financial fraud and criminals mostly attack on the person who shows their greed to have lots of money and this greed leads them the victim of a cyber crime.

viii). Lack of Awareness

One of the big reason for increment of cyber crime is also that people are still not aware of the ways of happening of cyber crimes and if they are a victim of the crime what steps should they take to get the justice. Even the police and the authorities are not completely aware of the way of cyber crimes and the ways to treat them resultantly the cyber criminals are ten steps ahead from the enforcement authorities.

ix). Acquiring of pirated data

Many of the people in India always try to get free things and they are using this habit in computers also as most of the Indians are downloading the pirated softwares, movies, songs etc. from an unknown and unsafe site only with a view to get that in free but at that time they save the money but let enter someone in form of virus, worm etc. who got the access in their system and affect them. This is also one of the biggest reason of increasing of cyber crimes in India.

X). Overuse of Smartphones

Smartphones are become the part of the life and the overuse of it leads increment in cyber crimes as people with lack of knowledge, clicks any links appeared on the social networking websites and app without verifying leads access of the attackers on their personal data as well as it is most commonly use for the committing of the crime pertaining to fraud and cyber pornography.

Chapter Five

Need of Cyber Law

The Information technology advanced by computer networks undoubtedly pervades every aspect of society and governance in the present new millennium with the increased dependence on e-commerce and e-governance, a wide variety of legal issues related to the use of the internet as well as other forms of computer or digital processing devices such as violation of intellectual property, piracy freedom of expression, jurisdiction, etc. have emerged, which need to be tackled through the instrumentality of law. Since, cyber space has no geographical limitations or boundaries nor does it have any physical characteristics such as sex, age, etc. it poses a big challenge before the law enforcement agencies for regulating cyberspace transactions of citizens with in a country's territorial jurisdiction. Though in practical terms, an internet user is subject to the laws of the state within which he/she goes online but this general rule runs into conflict where the disputes are international in nature. It is true that at the time when computer technology was in its developing stage no one ever contemplated that it could be indiscreetly misused by internet users for criminal purposes. Because of the anonymity of its character and least possibility of being detected, cyber criminals are misusing the computer for a variety of crimes which calls for the need for an effective legal framework and regulatory measures to prevent the incidence of this peculiar type of criminality which is rampant in cyber space.

And as time changes with increment in cyber crimes, there is a need for specific laws that only treated the offence regarding the cyber crime. In India there is only law which is specifically for cyber crime i.e., Information Technology Act, 2000 which amended in 2008. But due to various lacunas (discussed later) there is need of strict law to control the crime rates.

In today's highly digitalized world, almost everyone is affected by cyber law. For example:[1]

- Almost all transactions in shares are in demat form.
- Almost all companies extensively depend upon their computer networks and keep their valuable data in electronic form.
- Government forms including income tax returns, company law forms etc. are now filled in electronic form.

[1] www.indiancybersecurity.com

- Consumers are increasingly using credit cards, debit cards for shopping.
- Most people are using email, cell phones and SMS for communication.
- Even in 'non-cyber crime' cases, important evidence is found in computers / cell phones e.g. in cases of divorce, murder, kidnapping, tax evasion, organized crime, terrorist operations, counterfeit currency etc.
- Cyber crime cases such as online banking frauds, online share trading fraud, source code theft, credit card fraud, tax evasion, virus attacks, cyber sabotage, phishing attacks, e-mail hijacking, denial of service, hacking, pornography etc are becoming common.
- Digital signatures and e-contracts are rapidly replacing conventional methods ofbusiness transactions..

Technology per se is never a disputed issue but for whom and at what cost has been the issue in the ambit of governance. The cyber revolution holds the promise of quickly reaching the masses as opposed to the earlier technologies, which had a trickle down effect. Such a promise and potential can only be realized with an appropriate legal regime based on a given socio-economic matrix.

Chapter Six

Characteristics of Cyber Crime

The concept of cybercrime is very different from conventional crime and due to the growth of Internet Technology, this crime has gained serious and immediate attention as compared to traditional crime.

Cyber crimes have some unique and peculiar characteristics which may briefly be stated as follows:

i. People with Special knowledge

Cyber crimes can only be committed through the devices that come under technology, therefore to commit this kind of crime offender gains special knowledge on internet and computers to commit such a crime. The people who have committed cyber crime are well educated and have deep understanding of the usability of internet. A person without adequate knowledge of working of the computer system and internet cannot commit such a crime.

ii . Territorial Boundaries

In cyberspace, the territorial boundaries are reduced to zero. A cyber criminal can commit the crime sitting in any part of the world to other corners of world. For example, a hacker sitting in India hack in the system placed in United States.

iii. Virtual World

Cyber crime commits in the cyber space and the criminal who is committing this act is physically outside the cyber space. Every activity of the criminal while committing that crime is done in the cyber space and it has been well known as virtual world.

iv. Lack of Evidence

As the crime is committed in the virtual world and can be done in any part of the world without physical access to the place where offence has been committed or is being committing, due to which the offender is not easily traceable as well as due to lack of experts in the field of cyber subject it becomes very difficult to collect evidence of cyber crime and prove them in court of law.

v. No Identification

The cyber crime has been committed through a networking system like computers, laptop, smartphones etc. therefore there is no requirement for the user to disclose his actual identity as well as cyber criminals are as mechanized in their act as they commit the crime without disclosing their actual identity which safeguards them to remain out of reach of the law enforcement agencies easily and quickly.

vi. New Ways of Old Crime

Cyber criminals have such potential as they create a new way to commit traditional crime in non-traditional ways. For example, cyber terrorism, cyber fraud, money laundering, theft of data, cyber pornography, counterfeiting by using computer etc. are some of the traditional crimes which are now committed through electronic media.

Chapter Seven

Classification of cyber crime

Cyber crime is only a generic term in which a computer or a computer network is either the mode of commission or target for criminal activities. However, there are dozens of ways of the commission of cyber crime and many of the cyber crimes could easily fit into different types. For example, Hacking is a common crime in which computer is a tool and also a target.

The classification of cyber crime can be classified into various categories, such as the kinds of cyber crimes on the role of the computer as an object as well as a tool for its commission, classification based on the criteria of the victims of the cyber crime, classification based on the categories of the offenders and finally the classification of cyber crime on the basis of the content, which brings within its fold almost all the cyber crimes.

I. Classification based on role of computer in cyber crime:

The classification of cyber crimes can be divided into four general categories on the role of computers as below. There are many cyber activities which are falling under one another:

(a) Computer as the Target

It is defined as, "When a private or official computer system is attacked by the internet either manually or by other means". This activity generally called hacking, may involve erasing of data or programs, virus and worm attacks, logic bombs, infecting a computer with Trojan horses, defilement of web site, stealing of data, identity theft, phishing, denial of service attack, spoofing, social engineering, malware, vulnerability exploitation and terrorist activity threatening the critical infrastructure.

b. Computer as a Tool:

It is defined as, "Computer is used to commit traditional crime in a high-tech manner". E-fraud, embezzlement, forgery, black mailing, sedition, promoting enmity between different classes, and defamation. Other crimes committed on the internet, theft of intellectual digital property, stalking, gambling and money laundering are covered under this head.

c. Computer as incidental:

The third category relates to situations where use of a computer by a criminal is incidental. It may be used as a storage device. Here, computer is not needed for the criminal activity but may provide evidence of the crime committed.

d. Computer as Associate:

Another type of crime that falls under the purview of cyber crimes is the new version of traditional crimes that comes across as a result of a widespread increase in the availability of computers and information technology. Software piracy is an ideal example of this type of crime. It is only because there is a ready market due to large numbers of computers, where software piracy takes place. In this type of cyber,crimes, technological growth essentially creates new crime targets. Counterfeiting, copyright violations, theft of computer accessories, piracy in the audio and video market etc are some examples of these types of crimes. As, the internet and computer increase their presence in the global society, this type of cyber crime is expected to increase phenomenally over the coming years.

II. Classification based on perpetuators of cyber crime:

Another way of classifying cyber crimes is based on the profile of criminals. These are:-

a. Insiders:

Some studies indicate that more than half of the cyber crimes are committed by insiders who are close to the victim's life like family member, close friend, employee etc. Insider crimes include missing parts, software, improper login attempts, using of other people‘s identity and password etc.

b. Outsiders:

Most common outsider threats originate from hackers. Initially, it was more like fun and challenging to break a password and enter another person‘s computer system.

III. Classification based on victims of cyber crime:

Another classification that has been used is based on the targeted victims of the crimes. The types identified under this method are briefly discussed below.

a). Against Individuals:

i).Harassment via e-mails.

ii).Cyber-stalking.

iii).Dissemination of obscene material.

iv).Defamation

v).Hacking/cracking.

vi).Unauthorized control/access over computer system.

vii).Indecent exposure.

viii).Email spoofing

ix).Cheating and Fraud.

b). Against Individual's Property:

i).Computer vandalism.

ii).Transmitting virus.

iii).Net trespass.

iv).Hacking/cracking.

v).Unauthorized control/access over computer system.

vi).Intellectual Property crimes

vii).Internet time thefts.

c). Against Organization:

i).Hacking/cracking.

ii).Unauthorized control/access over computer system.

iii).Possession of unauthorized information.

iv).Cyber terrorism against the governmental organization.

v).Distribution of pirated software etc.

d). Against society at large:

i).Pornography (basically child pornography).

ii).Polluting the youth through indecent exposure.

iii).Trafficking.

iv).Financial crimes.

v).Sale of illegal articles

vi).Online gambling.

vii).Forgery

IV. Content Basis Classification of Cyber crime

The mode of commission of the cyber crimes is different than the traditional crimes. However, it has been seen that conventional crimes are committed by using computers. Besides committing cyber crimes through the instrumentality of computers, there are certain pure cyber crimes that are committed only in the cyber world. Various categories of cyber crimes are as follows:

a. Hacking:

Hacking is an attempt to exploit a computer system or a private network inside a computer. In simple words, it is the unauthorised access to or control over computer network security systems for some illicit purpose.

Hacking has been committed mostly for fun, for gaining limelight in public or to cause harm and earn some profit by stealing private information like credit card numbers, account numbers, confidential information stored either in emails or in the hard disk of computers for terrorism etc.

Unauthorised access has been covered under sec 43(a) of and punishable under sec 65 of Information Technology Act 2000.

b. Virus

A computer virus is a programme designed to replicate and spread, generally with the victim being oblivious to its existence. Computer viruses spread by attaching themselves to programme like word processors or spreadsheets or they attach themselves to the boot sector of a disk. Thus when an infected file is activated, the virus itself is also executed. Section 43(c) of the Information Technology Act covers the area of introduction of viruses, etc.

c. Trojan horse:

A Trojan horse is defined as a malicious, security breaking program that is disguised as something benign such as a directory lister, archiver, game, or a programme to search or destroy viruses. Trojans let a hacker access the victim‘s hard disk, and also many functions on his computer.

d. Logic bombs

Logic bombs detonated in a computer, make the program go into an infinite loop, crash the computer, delete data files, or some other damage to the computer or its data.

e. Worms

Worms are targeted at the larger machines-most usually, various flavors of UNIX – that are connected to the Internet. These programs are similar in many ways to the simpler viruses, by infecting a series of vulnerable computers. They differ, however, in that they rely on independently propagating copies of themselves to subsequent hosts, rather than on the actions of unwitting users.

f. Online Forgery:

Online forgery is an offence that needs little effort as compared to offline forgery. It is not usually restored to for money but it is also employed for glory or a spirit of evilness. Forgery is an offence that existed much before the Internet and in common law, it is defined as the fraudulent making or alteration of a writing to the prejudice of another man‘s right.

Computer forgery is the alteration of computerized documents. Since the proliferation of high-resolution computerized colour laser copies, a new generation of fraudulent counterfeiting has emerged.

g. Intellectual Property crimes:

Intellectual property consists of a bundle of rights. Any unlawful act by which the owner is deprived completely or partially of his rights is an offence. The common form of IPR violation may be said to be software piracy, copyright infringement, trademark and service mark violation, theft of computer source code, etc. With the development of the internet, such efficient telecommunication and information system has strengthened legitimate commercial activities in the present day global market which may also be easily used by criminal networks. This explosion of digitization and the internet have further enabled intellectual property violators to easily copy and illegally distribute trade-secrets, trade-marks, logos etc. Intellectual property is the physical expression of ideas contained in books, music, plays and computer software. Making copies of intellectual property including music, movies and software without the right to do so is punishable under the Copyright Act 1957.

i. Copyright Violation

Copyright is an intellectual property right that subsists in literary and artistic creations. But this right, when violated is not adequately protected and illegal unauthorized distribution of copyrighted works is often the common grievance of copyright owners. A copyright owner may place his work on the World wide web with the intention of sharing his creations with the public, but this is usually exploited by cyber criminals for their personal gain. Besides this violation of copyright, plagiarism is also rampant in the academic and literary world, therefore, copyright also seeks protection from plagiarism. Some aggravated forms of copyright violations are widespread in the business world. They are known as software piracy, industrial piracy etc.

ii. Protection of Trademarks

Trademarks are those intellectual property rights that protect a trader's goodwill and reputation and differentiate his goods from other traders in the same streams or business. Trademark infringement or passing-off actions typically arise through the use of marks by one person that belongs to another person. Thus, if a particular logo is generally associated with and used in relation to product A, its use by someone else in relation to product B, would amount to infringement of trademark right and it would be treated as an act of passing off which is punishable under the law of *torts*.

h. Cyber Fraud:

Cyber fraud is not defined in the Information Technology Act 2000 in India. However, according to D. Bainbridge, the phrase 'Computer Fraud' is used to describe stealing money or property by means of a computer that is using a computer to obtain dishonestly, property including money and cheques, credit card services, or to evade dishonestly some debt or liability. It might involve dishonestly giving an instruction to a computer to transfer funds into a bank account or using a forged bank card to obtain money from a cash dispenser i.e., an automated teller machine. As electronic commerce has become more prevalent, the application of digital technology to fraudulent endeavours is much greater. The term computer fraud denotes a sub-class of economic crimes that are being carried out with the help of a computer network and Internet in the cyberspace. The Internet has certain inherent features that make it ideal for fraudulent purposes: Cost-effectiveness, breadth of reach, difficulties in authenticating identity, anonymity, ease of personalizing appeals, and novelty. Online fraud is one of the most lucrative businesses that is growing today in cyber space. It may assume different forms. Some of the cases of online fraud and cheating that have come to light are those pertaining to credit card crimes, contractual crimes, offering jobs etc.

i. Cyber Terrorism:

Cyber terrorism may be defined to be the premeditated use of disruptive activities, or the threat thereof, in cyberspace, with the intention to further social, ideological, religious, political or similar objectives, or to intimidate any person in furtherance of such objectives. The convergence of Cyberspace and Terrorism is known as Cyber-terrorism. Cyber-terrorism is generally understood to mean unlawful attacks and threats of attacks against computers, networks, and the information stored therein when done to intimidate or coerce a Government or its people in furtherance of political or social objectives.

The role of a computer with respect to terrorism is that a modern thief can steal more with a computer than with a gun and a future terrorist may be able to cause more damage with a keyboard than a bomb. No doubt, the great fears are combined in terrorism, the fear of random, violent, victimization segues well with the distrust and out of fear of computer technology. Technology is complex, abstract, and indirect in its impact on individuals and it is easy to distrust that which one is not able to control. People believe that technology has the ability to become the master and humanity its servant. A cyber crime is generally a domestic issue, which may have international consequences; however cyber terrorism is a global concern, which has domestic as well as international consequences. The common form of these terrorist attacks on the Internet is distributed denial of service attacks, hate websites and emails, attacks on sensitive computer networks, etc.

Therefore, we can say even use of mobile phone, wireless, laptop, pocket PCs as well as the traditional concept of computers to commit terrorism or cause injury to those who cause terror in the minds of public and Government will be treated as cyber terrorism.

j. Cyber Warfare:

The cyber warfare has gained so much favor among military strategies that most of the armies of the world now have dedicated cyber warfare terms for defensive as well as offensive operations. Defence planners around the world are investing substantially in information warfare means of disrupting the information technology infrastructure of defence systems.

k. Cyber Pornography:

Pornography is defined as the sexually explicit depiction of persons, in words or images, created with the primary, proximate aim, and reasonable hope, of eliciting significant sexual arousal on the part of the consumers of such materials'. Pornography is distributed through different mediums, including books, magazines, movies, sounds, and animation. Internet pornography, or cyberporn, is the use of the internet (e.g., porno websites, peer-to-peer file-sharing networks, chat rooms, electronic bulletin boards) to distribute pornographic material. The presence of pornographic material on a public and global network such as the Internet raises serious concerns for parents, teachers, institutions, and governments. The Internet has provided a medium for the facilitation of crimes like pornography. Cyber porn as it is popularly known is widespread. Almost 50% of the websites exhibit pornographic material today. Pornography materials can also be reproduced more quickly and cheaply on new media like pen drives. The new technology is not merely limited to texts and images but have full motion video clips and movies too. These have serious consequences and have resulted in serious offences that have universal disapproval like child pornography which is far easier for offenders to hide and propagate through the medium of the internet. Pornography means polluting through indecent exposure. Cyber pornography is believed to be one of the largest businesses on the Internet today. While pornography per se is not illegal in many countries, child pornography is strictly illegal in most nations today. Pornography on the net may take various forms. It may include the hosting of the web site containing these prohibited materials, the use of computers for producing these obscene materials, and downloading through the Internet obscene materials. These obscene materials may cause harm to the minds of adolescent and tend to deprave or corrupt their minds.

l. Financial Crimes:

Money is the most common motive behind all crimes including most of the cyber crimes. Globally it is being observed that more and more cyber crimes are being committed for financial motives rather than for revenge or for greed. With the tremendous increase in the use of internet and mobile banking, online share trading, dematerialization of shares and securities, this trend is likely to increase unabated. Financial crimes include cyber cheating, credit card frauds, money laundering, hacking into bank servers, computer manipulation, accounting scams, etc.

m. Sale of illegal articles:

It is becoming increasingly common to find cases where sale of illegal articles such as narcotic drugs, weapons, wildlife, etc, is being facilitated by the Internet. Information about the availability of the products for sale is being posted on auction websites, bulletin boards, etc. It is practically impossible to control or prevent a criminal from setting up a website to transact in illegal article. Additionally, several online payment gateways can transfer money around the world at the click of a button. The Internet has also created a marketplace for the sale of unapproved drugs, prescription drugs, dispensed without a valid prescription, or products marketed with fraudulent health claims. Many sites focus on selling prescription drugs and are referred to by some as Internet pharmacies.

These sites offer for sale either approved prescription drug product or in some cases, unapproved, illegal versions of prescription drugs. This poses a serious potential threat to the health and safety of patients. The broad reach, relative anonymity, and ease of creating new or removing old websites, pose great challenges for law enforcement officials.

n. Online Gambling:

The habitual and professional gamblers have plenty of opportunities to satisfy their craze for gambling on the internet. There are millions of websites that offer online gambling. They offer online gambling where gamblers upload funds to the online gambling company, make bets or play the games that it offers, and then cash out any winnings. The rapidly growing number of online gambling sites clearly indicates that gambling has become a potential source of entertainment for the computer friendly person particularly, the youths though they may at times by duped, deceived, or cheated by some fake gambling sites. The special issue with online gambling is that it is legalised in several countries. So, legally the owners of these websites are safe in their home countries. The legal issues arise when a person residing in a foreign country like India (where such websites are illegal) gambles on such a website.

o. Phishing:

In computing, phishing is a form of social engineering characterized by attempts to fraudulently acquire sensitive information, such as passwords and credit cards, by masquerading as a trustworthy person or business in an apparently official electronic communication, such as an email or an instant message. The term phishing arises from the use of increasingly sophisticated lures to fish for users‘ financial information and passwords. Sending an email to a user falsely claiming to be an established and legitimate enterprise in an attempt to scam the user into surrendering private information they will be used for identity. The email directs the user to visit a website where they are asked to update personal information, such as passwords and credit cards, however is bogus and is set up only to steal the users‘ information. By spamming a large group of people, the phisher counted on the email being read by a brand spoofing or carding, is a variation on, fishing, the idea being that the bait is thrown out with the hope that while most will ignore the bait, some will be tempted into bring it. With the growing no of reported phishing incidents, additional methods of protection are needed. Attempt includes legislation, user training and technical measures. More recent phishing attempts have started to target the customers of bank and online payment service. While the first such examples are sent indiscriminately in the hope of finding a customer of a given bank or service, recent research has shown that phishers may in principle be able to establish what bank a potential victim has a relation with, and then sends an appropriate spoofed email to the victim. In general such targeted versions of phishing have been termed as spear phishing.

p. Cyber Defamation:

Defamation is defined as an intentional false communication, either published or publicly spoken, that injures another‘s reputation or good name. Defamation with the advent of computers where certain defamatory information is published or posted through email or chat rooms with an intention to defame the reputation of the person is called cyber defamation. Cyber defamation is not different from conventional defamation except the involvement of a cyberspace medium in the former. Sending defamatory email, writing derogatory comments on Facebook, Whattsapp or other social networking sites also constitutes cyber defamation. The internet can be used to spread misinformation, just as easily as information. Defamation can seriously injure the reputation and dignity of victims to a considerable degree, as online statements are accessible to a worldwide audience.

q. Cyber Stalking:

Stalking in general means behavior of harassing or threatening the other person. Cyber stalking is an extension of the physical form of stalking, which is committed over the online medium with the use of Information Technology. In cyber stalking the internet, e-mail, chat rooms etc. are used to stalk another person.

The wikipedia defines cyber stalking, as the internet or other electronic means to stalk or harass an individual, a group of individuals, or an organization. It includes the making of false accusations or statements of fact (as in defamation), monitoring, making threats, identity theft, damage to data or equipment, the solicitation of minors for sex, or gathering information that may be used to harass.

Stalking is a continuous process, consisting of a series of actions, each of which may be entirely legal in itself. The definition of cyber stalking is not universally acceptable as it varies from place to place.

r. Web Defacement:

Website defacement is usually the substitution of the original home page of a website with another page by a hacker. Religious and government sites are regularly targeted by hackers to display political or religious beliefs. Disturbing images and offensive phrases might be displayed in the process, as well as a signature of sorts, to show who was responsible for the defacement. Websites are not only defaced for political reasons; many defacers do it just for the thrill. For example, there are online contests in which hackers are awarded points for defacing the largest number of websites in a specified amount of time. Corporations are also targeted more often than other sites on the internet and they often seek to take measures to protect themselves from defacement or hacking in general. Websites represent the image of a company or organization and these are, therefore, especially vulnerable to defacement. Visitors may lose faith in sites that cannot promise security and become wary of performing online transactions. After defacement, sites have to be shut down for repairs, sometimes for an extended period of time, causing expenses and loss of profit.

s. Web Jacking:

Web-jacking is another form of hacking. This term is derived from the term hijacking. In web-jacking, the perpetrator forcefully takes control over the website of another with an identical motive of deriving ransom to accomplish is monetary or political purposes. This occurs when someone forcefully takes control of a website by cracking the password and then changing it. The actual owner of the website does not have any control over what appears on that website.

t. Salami Attacks:

A salami attack is a series of minor data-security attack that together result in a larger attack. For example, a fraud activity in a bank, where an employee steals a small amount of funds from several accounts, can be considered a salami attack. Crimes involving salami attacks are typically difficult to detect and trace. These attacks are used for the commission of financial crimes. The key here is to make the alteration so insignificant that in a single case if would go completely unnoticed. E.g. a bank employee inserts a program into the bank‘s servers that deduct a small amount of money (say Rs. 5) a month) from the account of every customer. No account holder will probably notice this unauthorized debit, but the bank employee ill make a sizable amount of money every month. This attack is called a —salami attack because some security specialists claim that it refers to slicing the data thinly, like a salami. Other argue that it means building up a significant object or amount from tiny scraps, like a salami.

u. Denial of Service Attack (DOS)

This is an act by a criminal who floods the bandwidth of the victim's network or fills his email box with spam mail depriving him of the service he is entitled to access or provide Short for denial-of-service attack, a type of service attack on a network which is designed to bring the network down to its knees by flooding it with useless traffic. For all known DOS attack, there are software fixes that system administrators can install to limit the damage caused by the attack. But, like virus, new DOS attacks are constantly being dreamed up by hackers. This involves flooding computer resources with more requests than it can handle. This causes the resource (e.g. a web server) to crash thereby denying authorized users the service offered by the resource. Another variation to a typical denial of service attack is known as a Distributed Denial of Service (DDOS) attack wherein the perpetrators are many and are geographically widespread. It is very difficult to control such attacks. The attack is initiated by sending excessive demands to the victim's computer, exceeding the limit the victim's server can support and making the servers crash. Denial-of-service attacks have had an impressive history in the past and have brought down websites like Amazon, CNN, Yahoo, and eBay.

v. Privacy Infringement:

The right to privacy is considered a fundamental right in almost all civilized world. The availability of information in cyberspace, for anyone with the capability to access, has brought up the issue of criminal infringement of privacy. Increasing use of computers and the Internet, people, knowingly or unknowingly store and transmit their data, which may be illegally accessed by capable offenders. Under section 72 of the Information Technology Act, 2000, where any person illegally and without consent of the person concerned discloses any electronic book, register, correspondence, information, document, or other material to which he got access under any of the provisions of the Act is any rule or regulations made under is liable for breach of confidentiality and privacy.

w. E-mail related crimes:

E-mail has fast emerged as the world's most preferred form of communication. Billions of email messages traverse the globe daily. Like any other form of communication, email is also misused by criminal elements. The ease, speed and relative anonymity of email has made it a powerful tool for criminals. Some of the major email-related crimes are as follows:

i. **E-mail Bombing:** Email bombing refers to sending a large amount of e-mails to the victim resulting in the victim's email account (in case of an individual) or servers (in case of a company or an email service provider) crashing. Sending numerous or large email messages to one person is considered e-mail bombing. Email bombing is characterized by abusers repeatedly sending an email to a particular address at a specific victim site. E-mail spamming is a variant of bombing: it refers to sending emails to hundreds or thousands of users. E-mail spamming can be made worse if the recipients reply to the email, causing all the original addresses to receive the reply.

ii. E-mail Spoofing

E-mail spoofing is a term used to describe fraudulent email activity in which the sender's address and other parts of the email header are altered to appear as though the email originated from a different source. Email spoofing is a technique commonly used for spam email and phishing to hide the origin of an email message. A spoofed e-mail may be said to be one. which misrepresents its origin. A spoofed e-mail appears to originate from one source but has actually emerged from some other source. Falsification of name and/or e-mail address of the originator of the e-mail is usually done by e-mail spoofing. Certain web-based e-mail services offer a facility where in addition to the above, a sender can also enter the e-mail address of the purported sender of the e-mail.

iii. Sending Malicious Codes through e-mails:

E-mails are often the fastest and easiest way to propagate malicious code over the internet.

iv. Sending threatening e-mails:

This is another way of committing a crime for ransom. With the advance of technology and frequent use of internet, it has become easier for criminals and gangsters to extract money from the victim by threatening him of his life for any other relative's life with the help of e-mail by sending it from any part of the world. Any person having a basic knowledge in any part of the world. Any person having a basic knowledge of computers or the use of internet can easily blackmail a person by threatening him via e-mails.

v. Defamatory e-mails:

E-mails are invariably used to send defamatory libel or slander against the victim in order to compel him to satisfy the lust of the criminal which may be either for money or for satisfying his illegal or unlawful demand or for avenging rivalry. Defamatory **e-mail** is an extremely fast and simple method of communication by which any kind of message can be sent to any person throughout the world, in a much more easier and effective manner. When one party makes a false allegation or statement by sending e-mail to another person that can harm that person's reputation, it is known as email defamation. An e-mail containing the defamatory material must necessarily be published. The publication is complete, sooner a person makes known or delivers the e mail containing the defamatory matter to another person, other than the person defamed. Thus publishing takes place merely for forwarding an e-mail to the third person, other than the person defamed.

vi. E-mail Frauds:

E-mail fraud may be defined as any fraudulent behavior connected with computerization by which someone intends to gain financial advantage for himself or for another person, thereby causing economic loss to the victim. There are many types of computer frauds and e-mail is a cheaper and popular devise for disturbing fraudulent messages to potential victims. With the development of global communication networks and computers, e-mail frauds are increasingly becoming a global phenomenon.

vii. Harassment via e-mails:

Harassment through e-mails is not a new concept. It is very similar to harassing through letters. It has become a concern for many people. This form of harassment includes directing obscenities towards others, as well as making derogatory comments based For example of gender, race, religion, nationality, and sexual orientation. This type of Internet crime can take place often in chat rooms, through news group, and even through the sending of hate emails to targeted mailing lists.

x. Data Diddling:

Data diddling involves changing data prior to or during input into a computer. In other words, information is changed from the way it should be entered by a person typing in the data, or a virus that changes data, or the programmer of the database or application, or anyone else involved in the process of having information stored in a computer file. The culprit can be anyone involved the process of creating recording, encoding, examining, checking, convening or transmitting data. This kind of an attack involves altering raw data just before it is processed by a computer and then changing it back after the processing is completed. Electricity Boards in India have been victims to data diddling programs inserted when private parties were computerizing their systems. This is one of the simplest methods of committing a computer related crime, because it requires almost no computer skills whatsoever.

y. Logic Bombs:

These are event dependent programs. This implies that these programs are created to do something only when event (known as a trigger event). E.g. even some viruses may be termed logic bombs because they lie dormant all through the year and become active only on a particular date (like the chernoby virus). A specie of malicious code which is conditional and dependent by nature causes breach of security at the commanded time and on the occurrence of certain conditions. It is formally defined as : a code surreptitiously inserted in to an application or operating system that causes it to perform some destructive. This virus was better known as I LOVE YOU (in may, 2000). This is a program which is used for targeting corporations, industries, etc. and to commit even a variety of traditional crimes like mischief extortion and can act either instantly or at a future date. As it targets chosen, systems a chain of destructions is hardly perceived, there by the loss is confined with in certain limits.

z. Trafficking:

Trafficking may assume different forms, it may be trafficking in drugs, in human beings, arms pseudonyms. A racket was busted in Chennai where drugs were being sold under the pseudonym of honey.

za. Computer vandalism:

Vandalism means deliberately destroying or damaging property of another. Thus computer vandalism may include within its purview any kind of physical harm done to the computer of any person. These acts may take the form of the theft of the theft of a computer, some part of a computer or a peripheral attached to the computer or by physically damaging a computer or its peripherals.

zb. Social Media

Social media is one the biggest platform for cyber criminals as in today's scenario many of the people are devoting their time to the social media and due to this they are easily get affect by cyber crime. On the Social media the cyber attackers are in attacking in various forms through phishing, influencing through fake news, photos, videos etc. and taking benefit of this cyber attackers are generating and increasing their activity on social media platforms.

Chapter Eight

Cyber laws in india

I.Information Technology Act, 2000

II.Information Technology Act, 2008

III.Indian Penal Code, 1860 (Amendment)

IV.Indian Evidence Act, 1872 (Amendment)

V.Banker's Book Evidence Act, 1891(Amendment)

VI.Reseve Bank of India Act, 1934 (Amendment)

VII.Cyber Security Policy 2013

I. Information technology ACT 2000

The Information Technology Act, 2000 in India is based on the Resolution[1] adopted by the General Assembly of United Nations on 30th January, 1997 regarding Model Law on Electronic Commerce earlier adopted by the United Nations Commission on International Trade Law (UNCITRAL). The UNCITRAL was created by the United Nations General Assembly by resolution[2] dated 17th December, 1966.

In India, Parliament has passed the first legislation which is specifically deals with cyber crimes the Information Technology Bill which having been passed by both the Houses of Parliament. received the assent of the President on the 9th June 2000. It came on the Statute Book as the Information Technology Act, 2000 (21 of 2000) (Came into force on 17-10-2000).

Preamble of The Information Technology Act, 2000 says "An Act to provide legal recognition for transactions carried out by means of electronic data interchange and other means of electronic communication, commonly referred to as "electronic commerce", which involve the use of alternatives to paper-based methods of communication and storage of information, to facilitate electronic filing of documents with the Government agencies and further to amend the Indian Penal Code, the Indian Evidence Act, 1872, the Bankers Books Evidence Act, 1891 and the Reserve Bank of India Act, 1934 and for matters connected therewith or incidental thereto;"

Further Information Technology Act, 2000 applies to the whole of India and also it applies to any offense or contravention committed outside India by any person.

The legislative provisions relating to cyber crimes are given under Chapter XI of the Information Technology Act, 2000 titled as 'Offences' which deals with the various types of offences which is done in the electronic form or concerning with computers, computer systems, computer networks. Strangely, the term 'cyber crime', or 'cyber offence' is neither defined nor this expression is used under the Information Technology Act, 2000. Hereunder, are mentioned those cyber crimes which are punishable under the Information Technology Act, 2000.

Salient Features of the Act are as follows:-

(i) Extends to the whole of India (Section 1);

(ii) Authentication of electronic records (Section 3);

(iii) Legal framework for affixing digital signature by use of asymmetric crypto system and hash function (Section 3);

(iv) Legal recognition of electronic records (Section 4);

(v) Legal recognition of digital signatures (Section 5);

(vi) Retention of electronic record (Section 7);

(vii) Publication of official gazette in electronic form (Section 8);

(viii) Security procedure for electronic records and digital signature (Sections 14, 15, 16);

(ix) Licensing and regulation of certifying authorities for issuing digital signature certificates (Sections 17 - 42);

(x) Functions of controller (Section 18);

(xi) Appointment of certifying authorities and controller of certifying authorities, including recognition of foreign certifying authorities (Section 19);

(xii) Controller to act as repository of all digital signature certificates (Section 20);

(xiii) Data protection (Sections 43 & 66);

(xiv)) Various types of computer crimes defined and stringent penalties provided under the act (Section 43 and Sections 66, 67, 72);

(xv) Appointment of adjudicating officer for holding inquiries under the act (Sections 46 & 47);

(xvi) Establishment of Cyber Appellate Tribunal under the Act (Sections 48 - 56);

(xvii) Appeal from order of Adjudicating Officer to Cyber Appellate Tribunal and not to any Civil Court (Section 57);

(xviii) Appeal from order of Cyber Appellate Tribunal to High Court (Section 62);

(xix) Interception of information from computer to computer (Section 69);

(xx) Protection System (Section 70);

(xxi) Act to apply for offences or contraventions committed outside India (Section 75);

(xxii) Investigation of computer crimes to be investigated by officer at the DSP (Deputy Superintendent of Police) level;

(xxiii) Network service providers not to be liable in certain cases (Section 79);

(xxiv) Power of police officers and other officers to enter into any public place and search and arrest without warrant (Section 80);

(xxv) Offences by the companies (Section 85);

(xxvi) Constitution of Cyber Regulations Advisory Committee who will advice the Central Government and Controller (Section 88).

II. Information technology act 2008

The Information Technology Act, 2000 in India is based on the Resolution[1] adopted by the General Assembly of United Nations on 30th January, 1997 regarding Model Law on Electronic Commerce earlier adopted by the United Nations Commission on International Trade Law (UNCITRAL). The UNCITRAL was created by the United Nations General Assembly by resolution[2] dated 17th December, 1966.

In India, Parliament has passed the first legislation which is specifically deals with cyber crimes the Information Technology Bill which having been passed by both the Houses of Parliament received the assent of the President on the 9th June 2000. It came on the Statute Book as The Information Technology Act, 2000 (21 of 2000) (Came into force on 17-10-2000).

Preamble of The Information Technology Act, 2000 says "An Act to provide legal recognition for transactions carried out by means of electronic data interchange and other means of electronic communication, commonly referred to as "electronic commerce", which involve the use of alternatives to paper-based methods of communication and storage of information, to facilitate electronic filing of documents with the Government agencies and further to amend the Indian Penal Code, the Indian Evidence Act, 1872, the Bankers Books Evidence Act, 1891 and the Reserve Bank of India Act, 1934 and for matters connected therewith or incidental thereto;"

Further Information Technology Act, 2000 applies to the whole of India and also it applies to any offense or contravention committed outside India by any person.

The legislative provisions relating to cyber crimes are given under Chapter XI of the Information Technology Act, 2000 titled as 'Offences' which deals with the various types of offences which is done in the electronic form or concerning with computers, computer systems, computer networks. Strangely, the term 'cyber crime', or 'cyber offence' is neither defined nor this expression is used under the Information Technology Act, 2000. Hereunder, are mentioned those cyber crimes which are punishable under the Information Technology Act, 2000.

Salient Features of the Act are as follows:-

i. The term **'digital signature'** has been replaced with 'electronic signature' to make the Act more technology neutral.

ii. A new section has been inserted to define **'communication device'** to mean cell phones, personal digital assistance or combination of both or any other device used to communicate, send or transmit any text video, audio or image.

iii. A new section has been added to define cyber cafe as any facility from where the access to the internet is offered by any person in the ordinary course of business to the members of the public.

iv. A new definition has been inserted for intermediary.

v. A new section 10A has been inserted to the effect that contracts concluded electronically shall not be deemed to be unenforceable solely on the ground that electronic form or means was used.

vi. The damages of Rs. One crore prescribed under section 43 of the earlier Act of 2000 for damage to computer, computer system etc. has been deleted and the relevant parts of the section have been substituted by the words, 'he shall be liable to pay damages by way of compensation to the person so affected'.

vii. A new section 43A has been inserted to protect sensitive personal data or information possessed, dealt or handled by a body corporate in a computer resource which such body corporate owns, controls or operates. If such body corporate is negligent in implementing and maintaining reasonable security practices and procedures and thereby causes wrongful loss or wrongful gain to any person, it shall be liable to pay damages by way of compensation to the person so affected.

viii. Sections 66A to 66F has been added to Section 66 prescribing punishment for offences such as obscene electronic message transmissions, identity theft, cheating by impersonation using computer resource, violation of privacy and cyber terrorism.

ix. Section 67 of the IT Act, 2000 has been amended to reduce the term of imprisonment for publishing or transmitting obscene material in electronic form to three years from five years and increase the fine thereof from Rs.100,000 to Rs. 500,000. Sections 67A to 67C have also been inserted. While Sections 67A and B deals with penal provisions in respect of offences of publishing or transmitting of material containing sexually explicit act and child pornography in electronic form, Section 67C deals with the obligation of an intermediary to preserve and retain such information as may be specified for such duration and in such manner and format as the central government may prescribe.

x. In view of the increasing threat of terrorism in the country, the new amendments include an amended section 69 giving power to the state to issue directions for interception or monitoring of decryption of any information through any computer resource. Further, sections 69A and B, two new sections, grant power to the state to issue directions for blocking for public access of any information through any computer resource and to authorize to monitor and collect traffic data or information through any computer resource for cyber security.

xi. Section 79 of the Act which exempted intermediaries has been modified to the effect that an intermediary shall not be liable for any third party information data or communication link made available or hosted by him if;

(a) The function of the intermediary is limited to providing access to a communication system over which information made available by third parties is transmitted or temporarily stored or hosted;

(b) The intermediary does not initiate the transmission or select the receiver of the transmission and select or modify the information contained in the transmission;

(c) The intermediary observes due diligence while discharging his duties. However, section 79 will not apply to an intermediary if the intermediary has conspired or abetted or aided or induced whether by threats or promise or otherwise in the commission of the unlawful act or upon receiving actual knowledge or on being notified that any information, data or communication link residing in or connected to a computer resource controlled by it is being used to commit an unlawful act, the intermediary fails to expeditiously remove or disable access to that material on that resource without vitiating the evidence in any manner.

xii. A proviso has been added to Section 81 which states that the provisions of the Act shall have overriding effect. The proviso states that nothing contained in the Act shall restrict any person from exercising any right conferred under the Copyright Act, 1957.

These are divided into two sections. The first section in which the punishment is in form of Compensation and the Second Section deals with the offence in which punishment is in form of Imprisonment or fine or both.

Section I

Right from the inception of The Information Technology Act, 2000, there was a provision under Section 43 providing for the contraventions which in term provided for the remedy in the form of compensation to the victim. Following is the provision which was in operation prior to The Information Technology (Amendment) Act, 2008.

Chapter IX Penalties and Adjudication Section 43: Penalty for damage to computer, computer system, etc. If any person without permission of the owner or any other person who is in charge of a computer, computer system or computer network,-

a) accesses or secures accesses to such computer, computer system or computer network;

b) downloads, copies or extracts any data, computer database or information from such computer, computer system or computer network including information or data held or stored in any removable storage medium;

c) introduces or causes to be introduced any computer contaminant or computer virus into any computer, computer system or computer network;

d) damages or causes to be damaged any computer, computer system or computer network, data, computer database or any other programmes residing such computer, computer system or computer network;

e) disrupts or causes disruption of any computer, computer system or computer network;

f) denies or causes the denial of access to any person authorised to access any computer, computer system or computer network by any means;

g) provides any assistance to any person to facilitate access to a computer, computer system or computer network in contravention of the provisions of this Act, rules or regulations made there under;

h) charges the services availed of by a person to the account of another person by tampering with or manipulating any computer, computer system or computer network,

He shall be liable to pay damages by way of compensation not exceeding ten lakh rupees to the person so affected.

For the purpose of the understanding certain terms quoted in the Section, the legislature has added the explanation to the said section. They have defined the terms "computer contaminant", "computer database", "computer virus" and "damage". The Information Technology (Amendment) Act, 2008 did not change the subclauses (a) to (h) in Section 43. By virtue of the Amendment in the year 2008, few more sub-sections were added under Section 43.

Section 43, right at the outset provides for the pre-requisites to enforce the liability under this Section. The two requirements which are discussed in the beginning of the Section 43 are:

I. The acts committed under this Section must have been committed without the permission of the owner or any person who is in charge of a computer, computer system or computer network.

II. There must be some kind of damage caused to the person affected by such acts.

Section 43 requires that, the act of default must have been committed without the permission of the person who is an owner or a person in charge of the computer, computer system or computer network. Secondly, the act of the defendant must have caused some damage or loss to the person so affected.

The provision of Section 43 of The Information Technology Act, 2000 provided eight different acts under Section 43 (a) to (j). Following are the acts which are prohibited under these sub-sections:

Section	**Offences**	**Penalty**
43(a)	Unauthorised Access	Compensation
43(b)	Unauthorised downloading, copying or extracting	Compensation
43(c)	Computer virus, worm, contaminant	Compensation
43(d)	Damaging a computer	Compensation
43(e)	Disruption of a computer	Compensation
43(f)	Denial or Cause to Denial Access	Compensation
43(g)	Assistance to Unauthorised Access	Compensation
43(h)	Internet Theft	Compensation
43(i)	Destroying, Altering, Deleting Information in Computer Resource	Compensation

43(j)	Steal, Conceal, Destroy or Alter Source Code	Compensation
43A	Failure to Protect Data	Compensation

Sec. 43 (a) – Unauthorised Access

Section 43 (a) provides for the very basic kind of an act which is prohibited under The Information Technology Act, 2000. If any person accesses or secures access to any computer, computer system, computer network or computer resource 26 without the permission of the owner or person in charge of such a computer, computer system or computer network, he is liable under this Section.

The Information Technology Act, 2000 defines "access" under Sec 2(a) as: "access with its grammatical variations and cognate expressions means gaining entry into, instructing or communicating with the logical, arithmetical or memory function resources of a computer, computer system or computer network."

The joint reading of the Section 43 (a) and Section 2 (a) clarifies that, if any person gains an access into the computer, computer system or computer network without the permission of the owner or person in charge, he is liable under this section.

It involves the entry into logical, arithmetic or memory function of the computer. These sections provide a blanket protection against any illegal or unauthorised access not only to computer, computer system or computer network but also to an unauthorised or illegal access as to logical, arithmetic or memory function in any resources of a computer, computer system or computer network. That means, if a person access the program files stored in a "C Drive" of a computer or laptop without accessing the actual data file created by the owner which is saved in "E Drive", still the person accessing the computer without the permission is liable.

The essence of Section 43 (a) is gaining an entry into any part of the computer either physically or virtually without the permission of the owner or the person in charge of the computer, computer system or computer network. The term „access" covers both physical and/or virtual access to a computer, computer system or computer network. The contravention under Section 43 (a) is a very basic contravention but is the one which is the most commonly committed in most of the cases of cyber crimes. To put it in more accurate terms, it is the initiation of all other serious cyber crimes or offences. The example can be cited in relation to Debit or Credit Card thefts. When any person accesses the Debit or Credit Card of another it falls within the meaning of illegal or unauthorised access. The theft may be proved at the next level, but initially, the person who secures access can be charged with unauthorised or illegal access.

Section 43 (a) initially only had the provision relating to unauthorized or illegal access to computer, computer system or computer network. The words „Computer resource" were added in to Section 43 (a) by virtue of The Information Technology (Amendment) Act, 2008.

This was an attempt to make wide application to the said provision under the Act. Earlier, the illegal access or unauthorized access could be committed only against the computer as a target or against the computer system which may involve the entire set up or computer network, which may be the network connections or anything which is connected with the computer. With the addition of the words, „computer resource", the data and data base or information residing within the computer also came within the purview of the application of Section 43 (a). This amendment in the said section signifies one more change in the approach that the illegal or unauthorized access is not only sought in the device but also in the data or data base or information residing in the computer.

Sec. 43(b)- Unauthorized Downloading, Copying or Extraction

Section 43 (b) is specifically meant for the protection of data, database or information from the copyright violation and even data theft. The advancement in the field of information technology has manifold the chances of creating multiple copies of any material stored in any computer, computer system or computer network. Information technology has posed many challenges to the intellectual property rights. Downloading, copying and extracting are the biggest challenges for all of them.

Sec 43(b) says that:-

"(b) downloads, copies or extracts any data, computer data base or information from such computer,, computer system or computer network including information or data held or stored in any removable storage medium;"

This section mentioned three things which are illegal if the data has been taken without obtaining permission from the owner or incharge of the computer, computer system, computer network i.e.,

i).Downloading;

ii).Copying;

iii).Extracting;

i). Downloading:-

The term downloading is not defined anywhere under The Information Technology Act, 2000. But technically, it means the access to the content of the data or information. It is the actual interface of the person to the information or data stored in the memory of the computer, computer system or computer network. For example If Ashish opens a MS word document stored in the computer of Sandeep without his permission, he has downloaded the document without the permission of Sandeep.

ii**). Copying:-**

Copying signifies the act of duplication of data or information. It is creating another copy of a document without hampering the original file or a document. Copying is serious than downloading.

Downloading merely is an act of procuring an access or opening a document whereas, copying involves an act of duplication of any data or information stored in a computer. For example: Vaibhav opens Ashish computer and put the pen drive in the computer. Vaibhav took some files in his pen drive. Vaibhav copied the files.

iii). Extracting

It is the serious most act than that of downloading and copying. Where copying involves only the act of duplicating or multiplying the copies of the data or information, extracting involves cutting the original source of the data and information and creating another source for the same information or data. The act of extracting involves the act which is popularly known as, cut-paste." In extracting, the original file is cut and is saved somewhere else. Extracting changes the source or path of the file. Extracting also involves retrieving a file from a remote computer, computer system or computer network and then selectively extract part of the digital content. For example Sandeep has made a project and compress the data to save from others. Ashish enters into the Sandeep computer in his absence and put his pen drive in Sandeep computer and convert the data of Sandeep compressed file into the executable file. Ashish had extracted sandeep file illegally.

The section also includes terms as Data, Computer Database, Information and removable storage medium.

1. Data means the quantities, characters, or symbols on which operations are performed by a computer, which may be stored and transmitted in the form of electrical signals and recorded on magnetic, optical, or mechanical recording media. Data can be in electric form For example songs stored in a CD or in a physical For example printouts of a computerized accounting system.

2. Computer Database means an organized collection of data, generally stored and accessed electronically from a computer system. It is a formalized representation of information.

3. Information means knowledge communicated or received concerning a particular fact or circumstance; news it includes data, text, images, sound, voice, codes, computer programmes, software and databases or Microfilm.

4. Removable Storage Medium is a form of computer storage that is designed to be inserted and removed from a system and the information or data has been stored in that even after removed from the computer system. For ex. C.D., Pen drive, Hard disk etc.

The essence of the act prohibited under Section 43 (b) lies in the unauthorized duplication of any data or information without the permission of the owner or the person in charge of the computer, computer system or computer network. The unauthorized duplication is definitely relates to copyright violation.

Section 43 (b) can be read with the Chapter XII and XIII of The Indian Copyright Act, 1957. Section 77 of The Information Technology Act, 2000 provides that no compensation awarded penalty imposed or confiscation made under The Information Technology Act, 2000 shall prevent the award of compensation or imposition of any other penalty or punishment under any other law for the time being in force.

Sec 43(C)- Computer Virus, Worm , Contaminant

Computer viruses are common to the entire digital world. A virus attack is the most common attack on the functioning of the computer. It is an attack on the logical functioning of the computer. It is a set of instructions or programme which destroys, alters or modifies the data or information residing in the computer. It adversely affects the logical, arithmetic or memory function of the computer. Virus may initiate certain instructions to the programme files of the computer which may involve the unauthorised sharing of the data or information to another computer or computer network. The effect of the virus causes damage to the data or information or even to the normal functioning of the computer.. It could be in the form of worms, Trojans or logic bombs.

The Information Technology Act, 2000 under Section 43 (c) makes an introduction of the computer virus or computer contaminant without the permission of the owner or person in charge of the computer a contravention. Sometimes for the purpose of creating anti-virus software, the companies need to introduce the contaminants and virus for the purpose of research and development. The most essential ingredient of the provision is introduction of the virus or contaminant without the permission.

Sec. 43(c) of Information Technology Act, 2000 stands as:-

(c) introduces or causes to be introduced any computer contaminant or computer virus into any computer,, computer system or computer network;;

Instead of making a segregation of all the types of the viruses, the Indian legislature has included one generic term for all of them and that is, computer contaminant. Under Section 43 (c) of The Information Technology Act, 2000, introducing or causing to introduce computer contaminant or computer virus without the permission of the owner or person in charge of the computer, computer system or computer network is treated as a contravention.

This section mentioned two illegal acts done by any person without the permission of the owner or in-charge of the computer, compute system or computer network. These are-

1).Introducing a computer virus or contaminant;

2).Causes to introduce a computer virus or contaminant;

Let us discuss the terminology of the section i.e, Computer Virus and Computer Contaminant:-

Computer virus defines in the **Explanation (iii) of Sec 43** of the **Information Technology act** as:-

(*iii*) "computer virus" means any computer instruction, information, data or programme that destroys, damages, degrades or adversely affects the performance of a computer resource or

attaches itself to another computer resource and operates when a programme, data or instruction is executed or some other event takes place in that computer resource;

This definition has two explanations stating as :-

"Computer virus" means any computer instruction, information, data or programme that

i)destroys, damages, degrades or adversely affects the performance of a computer resource: or

ii)attaches itself to another computer resource and operates when a programme, data or instruction is executed or some other event takes place in that computer resource;

Computer Contaminant defines in the **Explanation (i) of Sec 43** of the **Information Technology act** as:-

(*i*) "computer contaminant" means any set of computer instructions that are designed–

(*a*) to modify, destroy, record, transmit data or programme residing within a computer, computer system or computer network; or

(*b*) by any means to usurp the normal operation of the computer, computer system, or computer network;

This definition of 'computer contaminant' includes in its ambit set of computer instructions which modify, alter or destroy data or information. A computer acts as a servant to the person who sets the programme for the computer.

This definition of 'computer contaminant' includes in its ambit set of computer instructions which modify, alter or destroy data or information. A computer as device obeys as a servant to the person who sets the programme for the computer. It prima facie looks as if the computer as device is working in a non obvious way. But the way it works is controlled by the programmer by giving certain set of instructions.

Illustration: Vaibhav and Ashish are rivals employee. Ashish with intention to affecting the files of Vaibhav sent a link through E-mail infected with a worm. when Vaibhav clicks the link worm has been installed in Viabhav's computer which transmitted all the data into the Ashish computer. This is the example of Computer Contaminant.

Sec- 43 (d)- Damage or Causing Damage a Computer

The Information Technology Act, 2000 under Section 43 (d) provides the most generic provision which can be imposed in the cases of the damage caused to the computer, computer system or computer network as well as the data, database, any programme or information in the computer.

Sec 43(d) of **Information Technology Act, 2000** Stands as-

(d) damages or causes to be damaged any computer,, computer system or computer network,, data,, computer data base or any other programmes residing in such computer,, computer system or computer network;;

This section mentioned two illegal acts done by any person without the permission of the owner or incharge of the computer, computer system or computer network. These are-

i). Damaging ; or

ii). Causing to damage.

The **Explanation (iv)** of **sec 43** of **Information Technology Act 2000** defines the word damage as:

"damage means to destroy, alter, delete, add, modify or rearrange any computer resource by any means."

It includes damage to both hardware and/or software either done physically or through virtual medium.

One important fact of the provision under Section 43 (d) is that, it does not only provides for contravention in case of successful damage caused to the computer, computer system, computer network, data, database or programme residing in such a computer, but also an attempt to cause damage is provided as a contravention.

Any virtual or physical damage caused to the computer or any data or information residing in the computer is covered under the same provision. The contravention covered under Section 43 (d) is loosely drafted to make it applicable in any given situation where the computer is targeted by any means. Any damage caused to the hardware or software is also covered under the same provision. **For example:** Chetan and Ashish working on a project. With malafide intention Chetan switch off the light caused switch off the Ashish computer due to which the data of Ashish computer has been corrupted. Chetan direct damages Ashish Computer.

<u>Sec- 43 (e)- Disruption or Causing Disruption a Computer</u>

The provision under Section 43 (e) is again a very generic provision like that of the earlier provision under Section 43 (d). Disruption is any act which creates any small kind of hurdle in the normal operations of the computer, computer system or computer network. It may involve any amount of an act which causes any hindrance in the usage of the computer, computer system or computer network.

Sec 43(e) of **Information Technology Act, 2000** Stands as-

(e) disrupts or causes disruption of any computer,, computer system or computer network;

This section mentioned two illegal acts done by any person without the permission of the owner or incharge of the computer, computer system or computer network. These are-

i). Disruption ; or

ii). Causing to disruption.

Disruption means a break or interruption in the normal course or continuation of some activity, process, etc.

In general sense, "Disruption means breaking of the continuity in the work or activity."

Sometimes the acts are committed which may cause disruption to the hardware, For example, causing physical damage to the device or even the LAN or any wired device. The purpose of the provision under Section 43 (e) is to provide protection against those acts which may not necessary sound to be very serious crimes or offences against the computer, computer system or computer network but it is to provide protection against the damage caused to the computer, computer system or computer system in physical form. These are the acts which sometimes are comparatively less serious acts but do cause hindrance in the normal functioning of the computer.

The purpose of the provision under Section 43 (e) is to provide protection against those acts which may not be very serious crimes or offences against the computer, computer system or computer network but it is to provide protection against the damage caused to the computer, computer system or computer system in physical form. These are the acts which sometimes are comparatively less serious acts but do cause hindrance in the normal functioning of the computer.

Sec 43(f)- Denial or Cause to denial Access

The denial of access is one more type of an attack on the computers. In this, the act of denial can be committed in physical as well as virtual manner. If the lawful owner or the person who is authorized to access the computer, computer system or computer network is not allowed to access. It covers under sec 43(f) of Information Technology Act, 2000.

Sec 43(f) of **Information Technology Act, 2000** stands as-

(f) denies or causes the denial of access to any person authorised to access any computer,, computer system or computer network by any means;

This section mentioned two illegal acts done by any person without the permission of the owner or incharge of the computer, Computer system or Computer network. These are-

i). Denial of access to an authorised person; or

ii). Causes to denial of access to an authorised person.

Let us discuss about Denial of access:-

"A denial-of-service (D0S) means when legitimate users are unable to access information systems, devices, or other network resources due to the actions of a malicious act by a cyber criminal."

In Denial of Service (DOS) Services affected may include email, websites, online accounts (e.g., banking), or other services that rely on the affected computer or network. A denial-of-service condition is accomplished by flooding the targeted host or network with traffic until the target cannot respond or simply crashes, preventing access for legitimate users. DOS attacks can cost an organization both time and money while their resources and services are inaccessible

In general sense, “Denial of Service means to disallow an authorized person to use his/her computer, computer system or computer network.” For example Chetan requested Ashish to book his train ticket to Goa from his account but Ashish denies. Chetan having rivalry intention creates a computer worm which disabled Ashish account resultantly Ashish failed to operate his account. Chetan totally denied access to Ashish to his authorised account.

The denial of access can be physical access to the device, where the deliberate attempt is made on the part of the accused to conceal the device physically or causing damage to the device in such a way that, the person is not in position to access the computer, computer system or computer network. The virtual denial of an access is also covered under the same provision. When any person who is authorized to have an access to the computer, computer system or computer network is not allowed to have an access to same, that can also attract the provision under Section 43 (f). The denial of access to the computer, computer system or computer network can be committed by changing the password of the computer without the permission of the authorized owner or person in charge or even putting the passwords to the computer itself or any computer resource without the permission of the person authorized.

The denials of access attacks on the website are also common these days. These attacks are also committed by the terrorist organizations. The websites and servers of the government establishments are the frequent victims of the denial of access attacks. The person who is legally authorized to have an access is denied the access to the computer, computer system or computer network or even the computer resource by either changing and putting the passwords on the existing files in the computer or it is the physical intervention to detach the authorized user of the computer, computer system or computer network to deny the access to the same. **For example,** Chetan and Ashish are government contractors. Both are trying to get a government contract. Chetan with intention to get the contract contact Sandeep to help him to access the Ashish computer to get the Ashish quotation for the contract. Sandeep helped Chetan to access Ashish computer. Sandeep has provided assistance to Chetan to facilitate his unlawful access.

Sec 43(g) – Assistance to Unauthorised Access

The provision under sec 43(g) of Information Technology Act 2000 shows the intent of the legislature to provide for liability on the person who is assisting any other person in committing contravention of any of the provisions under The Information Technology Act, 2000, Rules and Regulations made there under.

Sec 43(g) of **Information Technology Act, 2000** stands as-

(g) provides any assistance to any person to facilitate access to a computer,, computer system or computer network in contravention of the provisions of this Act,, rules or regulations made thereunder;

This section emphasis especially to the person who gave assistance to access the computer, computer system or computer network to a person unlawfully in contravention of the provisions, rules and regulations of the Information Technology Act and its allied laws.

And the person who get that unlawful access to any computer, computer system or computer network is liable under relevant sections of the Information Technology Act, 2000 (Sec 43 (a), 66 or 77).

This section termed as:-

Assistance means 'to help' or 'to give aid' someone who is neither the owner nor the incharge to access a computer, computer system or computer network.

Facilitate means 'to make easier' or 'to make less difficult' someone who is neither the owner nor the incharge to access a computer, computer system or computer network.

Contravention means the act done by someone which is 'Against a law' or 'Against the provisions of law', or 'violation of the provisions of Law.'

Rules means a set of instruction which emphasis about doing of act and stoppage to do something.

The provision under Section 43 (g) gives a wide area of application as assistance in case of any contravention of the provisions of The Information Technology Act, 2000 or Rules or Regulations made under The Information Technology Act, 2000 is also provided.

<u>Sec 43(h) Internet Theft</u>

Internet Theft has nowhere termed in Information Technology Act, 2000 but it is directly connected with Sec. 43(h) of Information Technology Act, 2000 as Internet Theft means whosoever without the permission of the owner or any other person who is in charge a computer system or computer network, charges the service availed of by a person to the account of another person by tampering with or manipulating any computer, computer systems or network.

Sec 43(h) of **Information Technology Act, 2000 stands as:-**

(h) charges the services availed of by a person to the account of another person by tampering with or manipulating any computer,, computer system,, or computer network;

There are three major components for the said contravention under Section 43 (h), which are as follows:

1. Without the permission of the owner of the computer, computer system or computer network;
2. Charging the services availed to another account of another person
3. By tampering or manipulating with the computer, computer system or computer network

The first and the foremost requirement of Section 43 of The Information Technology Act, 2000 is that the act under Section 43 must have been committed without the permission of the person who is the owner or person in charge of the computer, computer system or computer network. Secondly, the contravention involves charging for the services to another person. This involves the contravention where one person has utilized any specific service but the other has been charged for the same even without the usage of the service by the person who is charged with it. This is common in the field of any service contract, where the subject matter involves some technical object, For example, electricity or telephones. Thirdly, the act is committed by tampering or manipulating the computer, computer system or network.

This section mentioned two illegal acts done by any person without the permission of the owner or incharge of the computer, Computer system or Computer network. These are-

i). Charging the services availed to another account of another person by Tampering;

ii). Charging the services availed to another account of another person by Manipulating.

The same logical analysis can be applied to the theft of internet hours and the person who charges the accounts on the services for another for the use of internet under the provision of Section 43 (h) of The Information Technology Act, 2000 can be subjected to the liability under Section 379 of The Indian Penal Code, 1860.

The Sec 43 (h) involves the contravention where one person has get any service from other person but that other has been charged for the same even if the person who charged for the service has not used for self purpose and the act is committed by tampering or manipulating the computer, computer system or network.

That this section emphasis especially for the person who is charging for availing the service to access one person who is neither the owner nor incharge of the accessed computer, computer network or computer system by either tampering or manipulation.

Let us discuss the terms used in the section:-

Tampering means the action of touching or making changes to something that you should not, usually when you are trying to damage it or do something illegal. For example Chetan enters into Ashish room where Ashish operates his computer. Ashish put a firewall in his computer to protect his computer. Chetan puts a magnet on the computer where the firewall was configured. Magnet corrupts hard disk of Ashish computer within few days which disables firewall of Ashish computer. Resultantly, Chetan easily access to Ashish computer unlawfully. Chetan tampers with Ashish computer.

Manipulating means to manage or influence skillfully, especially in an unfair manner. For example, Chetan receives an e-mail from Sandeep for winning one crore rupees in a lottery and sent a link alongwith e-mail. When chetan clicks on the link it request all the personal and bank details of Chetan. Chetan enters the detail and submitted. Sandeep got all the details from the Chetan and took 1,00,000/- from his account. Sandeep manipulated Chetan and liable under this section.

In the recent times, the provision under Section 43 (h) is becoming useful weapon for the prosecution in cases where Debit or Credit Cards are stolen and the amount is debited on to the account of the owner of the card. For example Sandeep receives call from Ashish. Ashish presenting him Sandeep as employee of bank and requesting the Card details otherwise his card will be blocked. Sandeep trusting Ashish gives his card details. Ashish mentioned that an One Time Password will be received to him and he needs to confirmation of the card details. Sandeep follows the instructions and gave one time password to Ashish and cut the call. Sandeep received message of debit of Rs. 50,000/-. Ashish manipulated Sandeep and liable under this section.

Sec 43(i)- Destroying , Altering, Deleting Information in Computer Resource

The major contribution of The Information Technology (Amendment) Act, 2008 was the introduction of contravention under Section 43 in the form of sub-clause (i) . The requirements as to commission of an act without the permission of the owner or person in charge of computer, computer system or computer network are also applicable to Section 43 (i).

Sec 43(i) of **Information Technology Act, 2000** stands as:-

(i) destroys,, deletes or alters any information residing in a computer resource or diminishes its value or utility or affects it injuriously by any means;

This section mentioned three illegal acts done by any person without the permission of the owner or incharge of the computer, computer system or computer network. These are-

i).Destroying/deleting/altering of information in computer resource;

ii).Diminishing value or utility of information in computer resource;

ii).Affects injuriously a computer resource.

The act of the person connoted under Section 43 (i) shall destroy, delete or alter the information in such a way that it may cause the diminution of value of the information residing in such computer resource and it must cause some loss to the person who is the owner of the computer, computer system or computer network.

Let us discuss terms mentioned in this Section:-

Computer Resource has been defined under Sec 2(k) of Information Technology Act 2000 as:-

(*k*) — computer resource means computer, computer system, computer network, data, computer data base or software;

Information means knowledge communicated or received concerning a particular fact or circumstance it includes data, text, images, sound, voice, codes, computer programme, software and databases or Microfilm.

Destroying means to damage something so severely that it no longer exists or can never return to its normal state or to put at end

Deletes means to strike out or remove or cancel or erase something written or printed. It can be temporary or permanent.

Alter means to modify or change in some particular as size, style, course, properties, format etc. It can be temporary or permanent.

Diminishes means to make or cause to seem smaller, less, less important, etc.; lessen; reduce

Value means the worth of something in terms of the amount of other things for which it can be exchanged or in terms of some medium of exchange.

For eg: Chetan worked in a company and prepared a excel sheet of all the clients who deals with the company and stored it in the computer as Information (This is computer Resource). That said information was very useful for the company and for security Chetan prepared a secure pen drive as the file can be opened when pen drive inserts into the computer. Chetan quits the job and took the pen drive with him but data is still in the computer resource. Chetan destroyed the information in the computer resultantly company couldn't made connection with their client because of which company's value has been diminished. Chetan destroys and diminished the value of information in the computer resource and liable under this section.

<u>Sec 43(j)- Steal, Conceal, Destroy or Alter Source Code</u>

The major contribution of The Information Technology (Amendment) Act, 2008 was the introduction of contravention under Section 43 in the form of sub-clause (j). The requirements as to commission of an act without the permission of the owner or person in charge of computer, computer system or computer network are also applicable to Section 43 (j).

Sec 43(j) of **Information Technology Act, 2000** stands as:-

(j) steal,, conceal,, destroys or alters or causes any person to steal,, conceal,, destroy or alter any computer source code used for a computer resource with an intention to cause damage ;

This section mentioned three illegal acts done by any person without the permission of the owner or incharge of the computer, computer system or computer network. These are-

i).Stealing, Concealing, Destroying, or altering of source code;

ii).Cause to Steal, Conceal, Destroy, or alter of source code;

This provision safeguards the person who is owner or person who is in charge of the computer, computer system or computer network from any act of stealing, concealing, destroying or altering or causing any other person to do the same, from the loss or damage caused to the computer programme, software or any piracy or copyright violation in the computer software. The provision under Section 43 (j) provides the protection for the most important technical attribute of any functioning of a computer or computer software and that is, computer source code.

Let us discuss the terms mentioned in this Sec:-

Computer Source Code has been defined under the same provision under Explanation (v) as :-

(v) defines "Computer Source Code" means the listing of programmes, computer commands, design and layout and program analysis of computer resource in any form.

In the common course of action if the computer source code is either destroyed or altered or tampered or manipulated, it will not be able to function properly. There will be a technical challenge as to the running of the computer altogether. If source code of computer gets damaged itself, that computer turns into a useless box.

Steal means to take (the property of another or others) without permission or right, especially secretly or by force.

In general sense, Steal meanse to commit or practice theft.

Steal and commit theft are used as interchangeably. Theft has not defied in the Information Technology Act, 2000. Theft has been defined under Sec 378 of the Indian Penal Code, 1860 as:-

378. Theft.—Whoever, intending to take dishonestly any moveable property out of the possession of any person without that per-son's consent, moves that property in order to such taking, is said to commit theft.

Whosoever has been done any act specified under this sec is liable to be punished under sec 379 of the Indian Penal Code, 1860:-

379. Punishment for theft—Whoever commits theft shall be punished with imprisonment of either description for a term which may extend to three years, or with fine, or with both.

Illustration: Chetan made a software program and take into a pen drive. Chetan left the pen drive into his system. Ashish took the pen drive without informing chetan. Ashish steals the pen drive and he is liable under this sec.

Conceal means to hide; withdraw or remove from observation; cover or keep from sight:

Illustration: Sandeep created a file and save it in his computer. Akash changed the name of the file the file has its document but due to change of name Sandeep cannot find his file. Akash Alter the information in the computer resource and liable under this section.

Destroying means to damage something so severely that it no longer exists or can never return to its normal state or to put at end

Illustration: Chetan worked in a company and prepared a excel sheet of all the clients who deals with the company and stored it in the computer as Information (This is computer Resource). That said information was very useful for the company and for security Chetan prepared a secure pen drive as the file can be opened when pen drive inserts into the computer. Chetan quits the job and took the pen drive with him but data is still in the computer resource. Chetan destroyed the information in the computer and liable under this section.

Alter means to modify or change in some particular, as size, style, course, properties, format etc. It can be temporary or permanent.

Illustration: Chetan created a file and save it in C Drive of his computer. Ashish changed the path of the file by cutting of file from C drive and pasting it into E Drive of the computer. The file has its document but due to change of Path Chetan cannot find his file. Ashish Altered the information in the computer resource and liable under this section.

Sec-43A- Compensation For Failure to Protect Data

The Information Technology (Amendment) Act, 2008 has inserted a new section 43A in the principal Act providing for compensation for failure to protect data. Section 43A of the ITA *inter alia* deals with protection of data in electronic medium[1] by providing that when an body corporate[2] is negligent in implementing and maintaining *'reasonable security practices and procedures'* in relation to any *'sensitive personal data or information'* which it possesses, deals or handles in a computer resource which it owns, controls or operates and such negligence causes wrongful loss or wrongful gain to any person, such entity shall be liable to pay damages by way of compensation to the person so affected.

The expressions *'sensitive personal data or information'* and *'reasonable security practices and procedures'* were not defined in the ITA, but are now defined in the Rules.

Sec 43A of **Information Technology Act 2000** stands as:-

43A . Compensation for failure to protect data: – Where a body corporate, possessing, dealing or handling any sensitive personal data or information in a computer resource which it owns, controls or operates, is negligent in implementing and maintaining reasonable security practices and procedures and thereby causes wrongful loss or wrongful gain to any person,, such body corporate shall be liable to pay damages by way of compensation to the person so affected..

Explanation . – For the purposes of this section,, –

(i) — **Body corporate** means any company and includes a firm,, sole proprietorship or other association of individuals engaged in commercial or professional activities;;

(ii) — **Reasonable security practices and procedures** means security practices and procedures designed to protect such information from unauthorised access,, damage,, use,, modification,, disclosure or impairment,, as may be specified in an agreement between the p arties or as may be specified in any law for the time being in force and in the absence of such agreement or any law,, such reasonable security practices and procedures,, as may be prescribed by the Central Government in consultation with such professional b odies or associations as it may deem fit;;

(iii) — **Sensitive personal data or information** means such personal information as may be prescribed by the Central Government in consultation with such professional bodies or associations as it may deem fit..

Let us discuss the important terms:-

Personal Information is defined under **Sec 2(i)** of **Information Technology (Reasonable security practices and procedures and sensitive personal data or information) Rules, 2011** as:-

(i) "Personal information" means any information that relates to a natural person, which, either directly or indirectly, in combination with other information available or likely to be available with a body corporate, is capable of identifying such person.

as well as **Sec 3** of **Information Technology (Reasonable security practices and procedures and sensitive personal data or information) Rules, 2011** has also describes about **Sensitive personal Data or Information**

3. Sensitive personal data or information.—

Sensitive personal data or information of a person means such personal information which consists of information relating to;—

(i) password;

(ii) financial information such as Bank account or credit card or debit card or other payment instrument details ;

(iii) physical, physiological and mental health condition;

(iv) sexual orientation;

(v) medical records and history;

(vi) Biometric information;

(vii) any detail relating to the above clauses as provided to body corporate for providing service; and (viii) any of the information received under above clauses by body corporate for processing, stored or processed under lawful contract or otherwise:

Sec 4 of **Information Technology (Reasonable security practices and procedures and sensitive personal data or information) Rules, 2011** has also describes about **Reasonable Security Practices and Procedures** have to be opted by the Body Corporate

8. Reasonable Security Practices and Procedures.— (1) A body corporate or a person on its behalf shall be considered to have complied with reasonable security practices and procedures, if they have implemented such security practices and standards and have a comprehensive documented information security programme and information security policies that contain managerial, technical, operational and physical security control measures that are commensurate with the information assets being protected with the nature of business. In the event of an information security breach, the body corporate or a person on its behalf shall be required to demonstrate, as and when called upon to do so by the agency mandated under the law, that they have implemented security control measures as per their documented information security programme and information security policies.

(2) The international Standard IS/ISO/IEC 27001 on "Information Technology – Security Techniques - Information Security Management System – Requirements" is one such standard referred to in sub rule (1).

(3) Any industry association or an entity formed by such an association, whose members are self regulating by following other than IS/ISO/IEC codes of best practices for data protection as per sub-rule(1), shall get its codes of best practices duly approved and notified by the Central Government for effective implementation.

(4) The body corporate or a person on its behalf who have implemented either IS/ISO/IEC 27001 standard or the codes of best practices for data protection as approved and notified under sub-rule (3) shall be deemed to have complied with reasonable security practices and procedures provided that such standard or the codes of best practices have been certified or audited on a regular basis by entities through independent auditor, duly approved by the Central Government. The audit of reasonable security practices and procedures shall be carried cut by an auditor at least once a year or as and when the body corporate or a person on its behalf undertake significant upgradation of its process and computer resource.

That from the above discussion it is cleared that there are two kinds of information is exempted from this sec. These are:-

i).Any kind of information which is easily available or such information is made publicly by the concern.

ii).An information availed under the Right to Information Act, 2005 or any law time being in force.

The provision under Section 43A of this Act clarifies that all body corporate, which are in possession of data and information of their consumers in their computer source, will implement 'reasonable security practices to prevent the unauthorized access to the personal data of their consumers. This section further entails that failure to protect the sensitive personal data of the individuals during the processing period by the company will make company liable to compensate the aggrieved person, whose personal data is so compromised.

Section 44 deals with the penalty for failure to furnish information, return etc. it imposes heavy penalties for different lapses on the part of any person who is required to furnish different information, documents and files, etc.

Section 45 of the Act deals with all such contraventions for which there is no separate provision for the penalty provided under suctions 43 and 44. According to the provision of this section, if a person contravenes any rules or regulations made under this Act and no penalty has been separately provided for such contravention, he shall be held liable to pay compensation of up to twenty-five thousand of rupees to another person who has been affected because of such contravention or in the alternative, he will have to pay a penalty up to twenty-five thousand of rupees. The penalty under this section is known as residuary penalty.

Section II

These are the sections of Information Technology Act 2000 which deals with the offence having punishment

Section	Offence	Penalty
65	Tampering with computer source documents	Imprisonment up to three years, or/and with fine up to 200,000
66	Computer Related Offences	Imprisonment up to three years, or/and with fine up to 500,000
66B	Dishonestly Receiving stolen computer	Imprisonment up to three years, or/and with fine up to 100,000
66C	Identity Theft	Imprisonment up to three years, or/and with fine up to 100,000
66D	Cheating by Personation Using Computer	Imprisonment up to three years, or/and with fine up to 100,000
66E	Violation of Privacy	Imprisonment up to three years, or/and with fine up to 200,000
66F	cyber terrorism	Imprisonment up to life.
67	Publishing or Transmitting Obscene Material Electronically	Imprisonment up to three years, or/and with fine up to 5,00,000 on first conviction. Imprisonment up to five years, or/and with fine up to 10,00,000 on second conviction.
67A	Publishing or Transmitting Sexually Explicit Act electronically	Imprisonment up to five years, or/and with fine up to 10,00,000 on first conviction. Imprisonment up to seven years, or/and with fine up to 10,00,000 on second conviction.
67B	Publishing or Transmitting Child Pornography electronically	Imprisonment up to five years, or/and with fine up to 1,000,000 on first conviction. Imprisonment up to seven years, or/and with fine up to 1,000,000 on second conviction.
67C	Prevention and Retention of Information	Imprisonment up to three years, or/and with fine.
68	Power of Controller	Imprisonment up to 2 years, or/and with fine up to 100,000

69	Interception, Monitoring or Decryption of Any Information	Imprisonment up to seven years and possible fine.
69A	Blocking of Public Access For Any Information	Imprisonment up to seven years and possible fine.
69B	Monitoring And Collecting of Data or Information For Cyber Security	Imprisonment up to three years and fine.
70	Protected System	Imprisonment up to ten years and fine.
70B	Indian Computer Emergency Response Team	Imprisonment up to 1 year, or/and with fine up to 100,000
71	Penalty For Misrepresentation	Imprisonment up to 2 years, or/and with fine up to 100,000
72	Breach of Confidentiality and Privacy	Imprisonment up to 2 years, or/and with fine up to 100,000
72A	Breach of Lawful Contract	Imprisonment up to 3 years, or/and with fine up to 5,00,000
73	False Electronic Signature Certificate	Imprisonment up to 2 years, or/and with fine up to 100,000
74	Publication For Fradulent Purpose	Imprisonment up to 2 years, or/and with fine up to 100,000

Sec 65- Tampering With Computer Source Documents

This is the first cyber crime which is punishable under the Information Technology Act, 2000. Section 65 makes provision to deal with the cases of tempering with computer source documents. The aim behind this section is to protect the intellectual property invested in the computer programmes. It is an attempt to extend the protection of computer source documents apart from what is available under the copyright laws.

Sec. 65 of **Information Technology Act 2000** Stands As:-

"Whoever knowingly or intentionally conceals, destroys or alters or intentionally or knowingly causes another to conceal, destroy, or alter any computer source code used for a computer, computer programme, computer system or computer network, when the computer source code is required to be kept or maintained by law for the time being in force, shall be punishable with imprisonment up to three years, or with fine which may extend up to two lakh rupees, or with both."

Explanation.-

For the purposes of this section, "computer source code" means the listing of programmes, computer commands, design and layout and programme analysis of computer resource in any form."

The essential ingredients of this sections are as follows:

1. A person should conceal, destroy or alter or cause another person to conceal, destroy or alter any computer source code used for a computer, computer program, computer system or computer network;

2. the computer source code should be required to be kept or maintained by law for the time being in force;

3. the concealment, destruction or alteration to computer source code should be done intentionally or knowingly.

Following are the various offences in respect of computer source code which have been covered by this section:

I. knowingly or intentionally concealing;

II. knowingly or intentionally destroying;

III. knowingly or intentionally altering;

IV. knowingly or intentionally caused another to conceal;

V. knowingly or intentionally caused another to destroy;

VI. knowingly or intentionally caused another to alter;

The idea behind the Section 65 of the act is to protect the "intellectual property" invested in the computer programmes. It is an attempt to extend the protection to Computers Source Documents (codes) beyond what is available under copyright laws.

In Syed Asifuddin and Ors V. The State of Andhra Pradesh (2205 CrLJ 4314) employees of Tata Indicom were arrested for tampering the electronic 32-bit number (ESN) programmed into the cellphones that Reliance Infocomm had taken exclusively through a franchise. The Andhra Pradesh High Court refused to accept the defence contention that since there is no law inforce which requires the maintenance if Computer Source Code." Section 65 of the Information Technology Act does not apply and the court opined that in Section 65 of the IT Act the disjunctive word 'or' is used in between two phrases:

1) When the computer source code is required to be kept'

2) "Maintained by law for the time being in force".

The court has held that ESN and System Identification Code (SID) came with the definition of 'Computer Source Code' under Section 65 of the IT Act. It has further held that such tampering constituted tampering with source code within the meaning of Section 54 of the IT Act, 2000.

This section clearly stresses on two words i.e. knowingly and tempering. It means a person shall be punished only if he knowingly or intentionally tempers with the computer source documents. If his act is unintentional, he shall not be liable to any punishment. As per explanation of to this section, the expression "computer source code" has been conferred with a very wide meaning which includes not only the listing of program, computer commands, design and layout, but also software programmes object code.

The offence has been penalised with imprisonment up to three years or fine upto two lakhs or both. The offence is bailable and Triable by the court of Judicial Magistrate First Class.

1. Syed Asifuddin And Ors. vs The State Of Andhra Pradesh [2005 CriLJ 4314]

Reliance model handsets were to be exclusively used by Reliance India Mobile Limited but the TATA Indicom staff members who were figured as an accused tampered with pre-programmed CDMA digital handsets belonging to Reliance Infocomm and activated with TATA Indicom network with all dubious means. Offence was held to be made out under Section 65 of IT Act.

2. Bhim Sen Garg vs State Of Rajasthan and Others. on 13 June, 2006 (2006 CriLJ 3643)

The Investigating Officer of FIR No. 217/2005 was concerned with the investigation of the offences under Sections 5 and 6 of the PITA Act and in the course of investigation when it was transpired that electronic report contained on the CD was tempered with and another CD was prepared by way of fabrication which was substantiated from the report of the State FSL, this constituted another and independent offence punishable under Sections 465, 469, 471, 120-B, IPC and Section 65 of Information Technology Act, 2000.

Sec 66- Computer Related Offences

By the Information Technology (Amendment) Act, 2008 'Data Theft' stated in section 43 is being referred to section 66 by making this section more powerful and the word 'Hacking' is not used. Before this amendment the offence covered under section 66 was 'Hacking with Computer System'. But now hacking is replaced by **Computer Related Offences**" which reads as:-

"66. Computer related offences.–If any person, dishonestly or fraudulently, does any act referred to in section 43, he shall be punishable with imprisonment for a term which may extend to three years or with fine which may extend to five lakh rupees or with both."

Explanation.–**For the purposes of this section,–**

(*a*) the word —dishonestly shall have the meaning assigned to it in section 24 of the Indian Penal Code (45 of 1860);

(*b*) the word —fraudulently shall have the meaning assigned to it in section 25 of the Indian Penal Code (45 of 1860).

These Sec. only gives the punishment of the provisions and act done under Sec from 43(a) – 43(j)

Section 43 of Information Technology Act states that:-

"If any person without permission of the owner or any other person who is in charge of a computer, computer system or computer network,–:-

a).Accesses or secures access to such computer, computer system or computer network or computer resource;

b).Downloads, copies or extracts any data, computer data base or information from such computer, computer system or computer network including information or data held or stored in any removable storage medium;

c).Introduces or causes to be introduced any computer contaminant or computer virus into any computer, computer system or computer network;

d).Damages or causes to be damaged any computer, computer system or computer network, data, computer data base or any other programmes residing in such computer, computer system or computer network;

e).Disrupts or causes disruption of any computer, computer system or computer network;

f).Denies or causes the denial of access to any person authorized to access any computer, computer system or computer network by any means;

g).Provides any assistance to any person to facilitate access to a computer, computer system or computer network in contravention of the provisions of this Act, rules or regulations mode thereunder;

h).Charges the services availed of by a person to the account of another person by tampering with or manipulating any computer, computer system, or computer network;

i).Destroys, deletes or alters any information residing in a computer resource or diminishes its value or utility or affects it injuriously by any means;

j).Steals, conceals, destroys or alters or causes any person to steal, conceal, destroy or alter any computer source code for a computer resource with an intention to cause damage.

As per the Sec the Section will apply only when the act discussed above done either dishonestly or fraudulently.

Dishonestly has not been described under the Information Technology Act but it has same meaning as described under Sec. 24 of Indian Penal Code. According to Sec 24 of Indian Penal Code, 1860:-

"24. "Dishonestly".—Whoever does anything with the intention of causing wrongful gain to one person or wrongful loss to another person, is said to do that thing "dishonestly".

Sec 24 of Indian Penal Code has defined two acts to be essential ingredients to be covered for the offence. These are:-

i).Wrongful gain; and

ii).Wrongful Loss:

Above mentioned terms has been defined under sec 23. of Indian Penal Code as:-

"23. "Wrongful gain".—"Wrongful gain" is gain by unlawful means of property to which the person gaining is not legally entitled. "Wrongful loss".—"Wrongful loss" is the loss by unlawful means of property to which the person losing it is legally entitled. Gaining wrongfully, losing wrongfully.—A person is said to gain wrongfully when such person retains wrongfully, as well as when such person acquires wrongfully. A person is said to lose wrong-fully when such person is wrongfully kept out of any property, as well as when such person is wrongfully deprived of property."

Fraudulently has not been described under the Information Technology Act but it has same meaning as described under Sec. 25 of Indian Penal Code. According to Sec 25 of Indian Penal Code, 1860:-

"25. Fraudulently.—A person is said to do a thing fraudulently if he does that thing with intent to defraud but not otherwise."

The word fraudulently consists two elements in a commission of crime:

I) deceit or an intention to deceive or in some cases mere secrecy; and

II) either actual injury or possible injury or an intent to expose some person either to actual injury or to a risk of possible injury by means of deceit or secrecy.

The offence under section 66 involves an invasion of right and diminution of the value or utility of one's information residing in the computer resource. Computer related offence involves mental act which destructive animus. It is the essence of this offence that the accused must cause destruction, damage, disruption, denial, deletion, concealment, tampering, manipulation, Stealing or alteration of information residing in a computer resource which was being owned, managed, used, or operated by any person, (natural or legal).

In **Abhinav Gupta. V State of Haryana, 2008 CrLJ 4536** An employee was alleged to have stolen confidential information and copyrighted material from his past employer and disclosed the same to his new employer. The code was of the view that such acts prima facie amounted to hacking under section 66 of. IT Act 2000 and rejected his bail petition as it did not accept his submission that the information was transferred in exercise of his duties.

The offence is penalised with imprisonment up to three years or fine up to Rs five lakhs or with both. The offence is bailable and Triable by the court of Judical Magistrate First Class.

Sec. 66A-Sending Offensive Messages

The offence prima facie appears to the head note of this section seems to be a substitute created for defamation.. It incorporated the words „sending offensive message"" is a crime under Section 66 A.

Sec 66A of **Information Technology Act 2000 Stands as:-**

66A- Punishment for sending offensive messages through communication service, etc.

"Any person who sends, by means of a computer resource or a

communication device,-

(a) Any information that is grossly offensive or has menacing character; or

(b) any information which he knows to be false, but for the purpose of causing annoyance, inconvenience, danger, obstruction, insult, injury, criminal intimidation, enmity, hatred or ill will, persistently by making use of such computer resource or a communication device; or

(c) Any electronic mail or electronic mail message for the purpose of causing annoyance or inconvenience or to deceive or to mislead the addressee or recipient tabout the origin of such messages,

Shall be punishable with imprisonment for a term which may extend to three years and with fine.

Explanation-

For the purpose of this section, terms "electronic mail" and "electronic mail message" means a message or information created or transmitted or received on a computer, computer system, computer resource or communication device including attachments in text, image, audio, video and any other electronic record, which may be transmitted with the message."

This Section penalise three acts if done by any person to be liable under this sec. These are:-

a)Sending or transmitting grossly offensive messages or menacing information

b)Sending information which causes annoyance,, inconvenience,, danger,, obstruction,, insult,, injury,, criminal intimidation,, enmity,, hatred,, or ill will

c)Sending misleading and annoying electronic mail or electronic mail message..

The first clause, Clause (a) of this section deals with the sending of information which is 'grossly offensive' or having a 'menacing character' such as online stalking, online defamation and text bullying, etc. But these two terms are not defined in the Act itself.

The clause (b) of this section deals with the sending of false messages with repetition for causing inconvenience like online insult, online intimidation, net extortion, hate mails etc.

The clause (c) of this section deals with spam and unsolicited mails such as e-mail spoofing and cyber phishing etc. Under this section the message may be in any form so long as it involves a computer resource or a communication device like e-mails, SMS's blogs, tweets, images, and voice over IP, Skype etc.

The offences like obscenity,, cyber stalking,, defamation,, bullying etc.. come under the ambit of this section..

On 24th March 2015 Hon'ble Supreme Court declared section 66A as unconstitutional and struck it down in **Shreya Singhal and others v. Union of India** considering it as a violation of Fundamental Right of Freedom of Speech and Expression Guaranteed under Art 19 (1) (d) of the Constitution of India and the misuse of the section by police in various states to arrest the innocent person for posting critical comments about social and political issues on networking sites.

The Hon'ble Supreme Court while struking down the Sec 66A of Information Technology Act held that

"it is clear that section 66A arbitrarily, excessively and disproportionately invades the right of free speech and upsets the balance between such right and the reasonable restrictions that may be imposed on such right."

Sec. 66B- Dishonestly Receiving Stolen Computer

Section 66 B of Information Technology Act, 2000 which is inserted by Amendment Act, 2008 deal with the cases of purchasing or receiving stolen computers or any kind of electronic or communication device from any person, whom he believes or any reason to believe that the device or computer resource was stolen.

The lawmakers have introduced an element of data protection IT Act by incorporating the Section 66B. Wrongful gain includes wrongful retention of 'intellectual property', rights 'of owners', data computer databases or information and wrongful loss included loss of 'intellectual property rights' vested in data, computer database or information as well as wrongfully deprived of such rights.

Sec 66B of Information Technology Act Stands as:-

"*Whoever dishonestly received or retains any stolen computer resource or communication device knowing or having reason to believe the same to be stolen computer resource or communication device, shall be punished with imprisonment of either description for a term which may extend to three years or with fine which may extend to rupees one lakh or with both.*"

Stolen property or **Dishonestly receiving stolen property** has been defined under sec 410 and 411 of Indian Penal code as-

410. Stolen property.—Property, the possession whereof has been transferred by theft, or by extortion, or by robbery, and proper-ty which has been criminally misappropriated or in respect of which 1[***] criminal breach of trust has been committed, is designated as "stolen property", 2[whether the transfer has been made, or the misappropriation or breach of trust has been commit-ted, within or without 3[India]]. But, if such property subse-quently comes into the possession of a person legally entitled to the possession thereof, it then ceases to be stolen property.

411. Dishonestly receiving stolen property.—Whoever dishonestly receives or retains any stolen property, knowing or having reason to believe the same to be stolen property, shall be punished with imprisonment of either description for a term which may extend to three years, or with fine, or with both.

The essential ingredients of this section are as follows:-

i).Receiving or retaining of computer resource after having a reason to believe that the computer resource is stolen;

ii).Receiving or retaining of communication device after having a reason to believe that the communication device is stolen.

Illustration: Chetan stole cell phone and offers Ashish to buy that phone for his half price as the phone is stole. Ashish bought the phone from chetan after have believe that it is a stoled cell phone. Ashish is liable under this section.

It would apply to those people who buy or retain stolen computer resource or any communication device. For the ambit of this section it includes devices such as mobile phones, laptops, and computers and also in the other computer resources such as stolen data and software.

The offence has been penalised with imprisonment up to three years or fine up to one lakhs or with both. The offence is bailable, cognizable and triable by the court of Judicial Magistrate First Class.

Sec. 66C- Identity Theft

Section 66C of Information Technology Act, 2000 which is inserted by Amendment Act, 2008 deal with stealing some other person's identity in order to commit crime, as per the provision of this section the person has to use other person's identity i.e. electronic signature, password or any other identification feature of other person dishonestly or fraudulently.

Section 66C of IT Act Treats 'identity' of a person as his authenticating feature and whoever, intending to take such an 'identity' dishonestly or fraudulently out of the possession of any such person is committing an offence. This section is about the loss of movable property, which may be in the form of electronic signature, password or any other unique identification feature of any such affected person. Further, it protects integrity and security of computer resource from attacks by unauthorised person seeking to enter such resources, whatever may be their intention or motive.

Section 66C of IT Act is meant to protect all e-commerce and e-governance services users in the online medium. The object of this section is to protect the privacy of all or any online users, including their personal information and data.

Sec 66C of **Information Technology Act** stands as:-

"Whoever, fraudulently or dishonestly make use of the electronic signature, password or any other unique identification feature of any other person, shall be punished with imprisonment of either description for a term which may extend to three years and shall also be liable to fine which may extend to rupees one lakh."

Theft has been defined under section 378 of Indian Penal Code, 1860 as-

378. Theft.—Whoever, intending to take dishonestly any moveable property out of the possession of any person without that per-son's consent, moves that property in order to such taking, is said to commit theft.

Explanation 1.—A thing so long as it is attached to the earth, not being movable property, is not the subject of theft; but it becomes capable of being the subject of theft as soon as it is severed from the earth.

Explanation 2.—A moving effected by the same act which affects the severance may be a theft.

Explanation 3.—A person is said to cause a thing to move by removing an obstacle which prevented it from moving or by sepa-rating it from any other thing, as well as by actually moving it.

Explanation 4.—A person, who by any means causes an animal to move, is said to move that animal, and to move everything which, in consequence of the motion so caused, is moved by that animal.

Explanation 5.—The consent mentioned in the definition may be express or implied, and may be given either by the person in possession, or by any person having for that purpose authority either express or implied.

The definition of the words dishonestly and fraudulently is explained in the Indian Penal Code, 1860, section 24 and 25 respectively have been explained previously to mean an intention to cause economic loss or gain to a person, and the intention to cause loss through deception respectively.

The Essential ingredient of this section are as follows:-

i).Someone having fraudulently or dishonestly intention making use of **electronic signature** of another person.

ii).Someone having fraudulently or dishonestly intention making use of **password** of another person.

iii).Someone having fraudulently or dishonestly intention making use of any **unique identification feature** (PIN, photograph, biometric identifier) of another person.

Identity theft may be in the form of :-

Financial Identity theft which consists of using stolen identity for financial fraud like extracted online banking details through phishing and used it to make purchases or transferring money ATM fraud is best example of it;

Criminal Identity theft consists of using of identity of other person for doing criminal activities like using another person's email for sending spam.

Commercial Identity theft includes the theft of identity of a company, business or other commercial enterprises for taking benefit or committing crime

This section does not differentiate between a natural person and legal person like a company.

The offence has been penalised with imprisonment up to three years or fine up to one lakh or with both. The offence is bailable, cognizable and triable by the court of Judicial Magistrate First Class.

Sec 66D- Cheating By Personation Using Computer

Section 66 D is inserted by Information Technology (Amendment) Act, 2008 for providing punishment for cheating by personation by using computer resource it means somebody pretends himself to be some other person or representative of that person to some person with other with the help of computer device or through online medium.

Sec 66D of Information Technology Act 2000 Stands as :-

Whoever, by means of any communication device or computer resource cheats by personation, shall be punished with imprisonment of either description for a term which may extend to three years and shall also be liable to fine which may extend to one lakh rupees.

Cheating has been defined under sec 415 and Cheating by Personation has been defined under sec 416 of Indian Penal code 1860 as:-

415. Cheating- Whoever, by deceiving any person, fraudulently or dishonestly induces the person so deceived to deliver any proper-ty to any person, or to consent that any person shall retain any property, or intentionally induces the person so deceived to do or omit to do anything which he would not do or omit if he were not so deceived, and which act or omission causes or is likely to cause damage or harm to that person in body, mind, reputation or property, is said to "cheat".

Explanation.—A dishonest concealment of facts is a deception within the meaning of this section

416. Cheating by personation.—A person is said to "cheat by personation" if he cheats by pretending to be some other person, or by knowingly substituting one person for another, or representing that he or any other person is a person other than he or such other person really is.

Explanation.—The offence is committed whether the individual personated is a real or imaginary person.

The essential ingredient of this section are as follows:-

i).Someone cheats by representing himself to be other person or representative of that person to some other person through communication device;

ii).Someone cheats by representing himself to be other person or representative of that person to some other person through computer resource;

The offence has been penalised with imprisonment up to three years or fine up to one lakh or with both. The offence is bailable, cognizable and triable by the court of Judicial Magistrate First Class.

Sec 66E- Violation of Privacy

Section 66 E is inserted by Information Technology (Amendment) Act, 2008 for providing punishment for violation of privacy deal with violation of bodily piracy, the person said to be committed the offense under this section when he/she intentionally or knowingly, capture, transmits or publishes the image of a private area of the person without his/her consent.

Sec 66E of Information Technology Act 2000 stands as:-

Whoever, intentionally or knowingly captures, publishes or transmits the image of a private area of any person without his or her consent, under circumstances violating the privacy of that person, shall be punished with imprisonment which may extend to three years or with fine not exceeding two lakh rupees, or with both.

Explanation.–For the purposes of this section–

(*a*) —transmit means to electronically send a visual image with the intent that it be viewed by a person or person;

(*b*) —capture, with respect to an image, means to videotape, photograph, film or record by any means;

(*c*) —private area‖ means the naked or undergarment clad genitals, public area, buttocks or female breast:

(*d*) —publishes means reproduction in the printed or electronic form and making it available for public;

(*e*) —under circumstances violating privacy‖ means circumstances in which a person can have a reasonable expectation that–

i).he or she could disrobe in privacy, without being concerned that an image of his private area was being captured; or

(*ii*)any part of his or her private area would not be visible to the public, regardless of whether that person is in a public or private place.

The essential ingredients of this Section are as follows:-

i).Any person intentionally or knowingly captures image of a private area of any person without his/her consent;

ii).Any person intentionally or knowingly publishes image of a private area of any person without his/her consent;

iii).Any person intentionally or knowingly transmits image of a private area of any person without his/her consent.

iv).Any person does the act with intention to violates the privacy of the person.

This section applies to the violation of the bodily privacy of any person by three stages i.e. capture, publication and transmission.

This section penalise any of these stages that are done without the consent of the victim

i).Capturing an image by any means such as videotaping, filming or recording by using any kind of technology like video recorders, cameras, CCTVs, webcam in a PC or any other forms of electronic surveillance like spy cameras or any kind of hidden cameras, smart phones etc.

ii).Publishing the creation of copies both in print i.e. magazines, books, newspapers and in an electronic form i.e. on the websites or CDs.

ii).Transmitting deliberate or intentional electronic transfer of the image via emails, internet, messaging, Bluetooth etc.

The offences which are punishable under section 66E include installation of spy cams/hidden cameras/communication device inside washrooms, bedrooms, changing rooms, hotel rooms, etc. for the purpose of violating bodily privacy of any user/occupant of such places.

Sting operation by a private person or an agency which may result in violating bodily privacy of another person will fall under section 66E of the IT Act. Whatever may be the reason, public interest or the people right to know, one should not disregard the protection being given to an individual against his bodily privacy under section 66E of the IT Act. A sting operation by State actor is also unacceptable if the State actor commits an offence so that an offence by another person is detected. However, State actor or a law enforcement agency may resort to hidden camera or string operations only to collect further or conclusive evidence as regards the criminality of a person who is already suspected of a crime with the prior sanction of an appropriate authority. The law enforcement agency must maintain the original version of the actual sting operation.

The offence has been penalised with imprisonment up to three years or fine up to two lakhs or with both. The offence is bailable, cognizable and triable by the court of Judicial Magistrate First Class.

Sec 66F- Cyber Terrorism

Information Technology (Amendment) Act, 2008 made the provision for cyber terrorism under section 66F which provides punishment for cyber terrorism.

The FBI defined Cyber Terrorism, "the premeditated, politically motivated attack against intonations computer system, computer programs and data which results in violence against non combatant targets by sub national groups or clandestine agents".

Generically, cyber terrorism consists of using computer technology to engage in terrorist activity.

Sec 66F of Information Technology Act 2000 stands as:-

(*1*) Whoever,–

(*A*) with intent to threaten the unity, integrity, security or sovereignty of India or to strike terror in the people or any section of the people by–

(*i*) denying or cause the denial of access to any person authorised to access computer resource; or

(*ii*) attempting to penetrate or access a computer resource without authorisation or exceeding authorised access; or

(*iii*) introducing or causing to introduce any computer contaminant, and by means of such conduct causes or is likely to cause death or injuries to person or damage to or destruction of property or disrupts or knowing that it is likely to cause damage or disruption of supplies or services essential to the life of the community or adversely affect the critical information infrastructure specified under section 70; or

(*B*) knowingly or intentionally penetrates or accesses a computer resource without authorisation or exceeding authorised access, and by means of such conduct obtains access to information, data or computer data base that is restricted for reasons of the security of the State or foreign relations; or any restricted information, data or computer data base, with reasons to believe that such information, data or computer data base so obtained may be used to cause or likely to cause injury to the interests of the sovereignty and integrity of India, the security of the State, friendly relations with foreign States, public order, decency or morality, or in relation to contempt of court, defamation or incitement to an offence, or to the advantage of any foreign nation, group of individuals or otherwise, commits the offence of cyber terrorism.

(*2*) Whoever commits or conspires to commit cyber terrorism shall be punishable with imprisonment which may extend to imprisonment for life.

The essential ingredient of this section are as follows:-

i).With intent to threaten the unity, integrity, security or sovereignty of India cause or likely to cause

a). death or injuries of person; or

b). damage to property; or

c). destruction of property; or

d). disruption of supplies or services essential to the life or a community; or

e). adversely affect the critical information infrastructure specified under sec 70 by means of:-

a). denial of access to computer resource; or

b). accessing or attempting to penetrate a computer resource without authorization; or

c). introduce or cause to introduce any computer contaminant.

ii).Any person gets unauthorised access to the information restricted in the interest of Security of the State;

iii).Any person gets unauthorised access to the information with intention to cause injury to

a). integrity and sovereignty of India;

b). Security of the state;

c). friendly relations with foreign states;

d). public order;

e). decency;

f). morality

iv).Any person gets unauthorised access to the information with intention that such information may leads:-

a). Contempt of Court;

b). defamation;

c). incitement to an offence;

d). advantage of any foreign nation or groups of individuals

The offence has been penalised with life imprisonment. The offence is Non-bailable, and triable by the court of Session.

Sec 67- Publishing or Transmitting Obscene Material Electronically

Section 67 of Information Technology Act, 2000 amended by Information Technology (Amendment) Act, 2008 deals with the publishing of information, which is obscene in electronic form.

Section 67 of the IT Act advocates that the 'obscene material in electronic form' must be considered by itself and separately to find out whether it is so gross and its obscenity so decided that it is likely to deprive and corrupt those whose minds are open to influences of this sort and into whose hands the 'obscene material in electronic form is likely fall.'

In terms of everyday application, section 67 of the IT Act will cover websites, graphic files such as GIF and JPEG, images (download from FTP sites, embedded in web pages), test messages (E-mail, SMS, chat room, BBS), Audio/Sound Messages (Net Telephony, Music Downloads), Digital Photographs (MMS, PNG or JPG Digital Photo Formats), Pseudo-Photograph (Morphed Images) Software Programmes, etc.

Sec 67 of Information Technology Act stands as :-

Whoever publishes or transmits or causes to be published or transmitted in the electronic form, any material which is lascivious or appeals to the prurient interest or if its effect is such as to tend to deprave and corrupt person who are likely, having regard to all relevant circumstances, to read, see or hear the matter contained or embodied in it, shall be punished on first conviction with imprisonment of either description for a term which may extend to three years and with fine which may extend to five lakh rupees and in the event of second or subsequent conviction with imprisonment of either description for a term which may extend to five years and also with fine which may extend to ten lakh rupees.

This section deals with Pornography publishing or transmitting through electronic form

Obscene means relating to materials that can be regulated or criminalized because their depiction of nudity, sex, or excretion is patently offensive and without artistic or scientific value.

Pornography means to describe or to show sexual acts with the intention to cause sexual excitement through pornographic websites or pornographic material produced by using computers, internet and also including to download and transmit pornographic videos, pictures, photos, writings etc.

Publish simply means "to make public or make known to the public, to make generally accessible or available; to place before or offer to public; to bring before the public for sale or distribution."

Transmit means "to cause to be conveyed to another person or place; cause to pass on from one place or person to another; broadcast or send out; allow passing through a medium."

Electronic form means with reference to information means any information generated, sent, received or stored in media, magnetic, optical, computer memory, micro film, computer generated micro fiche or similar device.

The essential ingredients of this section are as follows:-

1.Publication or transmission or an act to be caused must be in electronic form.

2.Publication or transmission or an act to be caused must be obscene i.e., lascivious or excite lust in nature.

3.Publication or transmission or an act to be caused must be appeal to the prurient interest i.e., arose interest in lustful thoughts.

4.Publication or transmission or an act to be caused leads its effect is such as to tend to deprave and corrupt person who are likely, having regard to all relevant circumstances, to read, see or hear the matter contained or embodied in it to become morally bad.

Exception-

section 67 does not extend to any book, pamphlet, paper, writing, drawing, painting representation or figure in electronic form–

(*i*) the publication of which is proved to be justified as being for the public good on the ground that such book, pamphlet, paper, writing, drawing, painting representation or figure is the interest of science, literature, art or learning or other objects of general concern; or

(*ii*) which is kept or used for *bona fide* heritage or religious purposes.

In Avinash Bajaj versus state ((2008) DLT 769) (The Baazee Case). The court observed that "the listing here was carried by the website baazee.com. The text of the listing leave no doubt that the object being offered for sale was obscene. By not having appropriate filters that could have detected the words in the listing or the pornographic content of what was being offered for sale, the website ran a risk of having imputed to it the knowledge that such an object was infact obscene. These are the attendant risk that a website owner attract when he exploit cyberspace for profits. The proliferation of the internet and the possibility of a wide spread use through instant transmission of pornographic material, calls for a strict standard having to be insisted upon. Owners or operators of website that offer space for listing might have to employ content filters if they want to prove that they did not knowingly permit the use of their website for sale of pornographic material.

The court opined for the purpose of section 67 of the IT Act, "whether the website caused the publishing of such obscene material. For this purpose, the chain of transaction is relevant. Once the interested buyer gets on the baazee.com and views the listing, he then opts to buy the said product and then makes payment. Only then the remaining part of the chain is complete and the product, which in this case is the video clip in the electronic form is then transmitted to an e-mail attachment and then can get further transmitted from one person to another. The video clip sent as an e-mail attachment can straight away be downloaded onto the buyers hard disc and numerous copies thereof can be made for further transmission. The 'publishing' in this form is therefore instantaneous and can be repeated manifold. In fact, in the present case, the transmission of the clip to eight buyers located in different parts of the country took place in a very short span of time. Therefore, it cannot be said that. baazee.com in this case did not even prime facie 'cause' the publication of the obscene material. The ultimate transmission of the video clip might be through the seller to the buyer but in a fully automated system that link of the transaction cannot take place unless all the previous step of registration with the website and making payment take place. It is a continuous chain. When five to six links of the chain are under the direct control of the website and it is only on completion of each step that the final two steps which result in the actual publication of the obscene material, ensure, it cannot be said that the website did not even prima facie cause publication of the obscene material.

The offence has been penalised with imprisonment up to three years and fine up to five lakhs or with both on first conviction and imprisonment up to five years or fine up to ten lakhs or with both on second conviction. The offence is bailable, cognizable and triable by the court of Judicial Magistrate First Class.

1. Avnish Bajaj vs State, famously known as Bazee.com case (2005)

CEO of E-Commerce Portal was arrested and given bail later under Section 67 of IT Act on account of an obscene video uploaded on Bazee.com for sale. He proved Due Diligence but in 2005, Information Technology Act did not have any provisions related to 'Intermediary' !

2. Sharat Babu Digumarti vs State, Govt. of NCT of Delhi (Bazee.com Case, Appeal)

Petitioner was working as Senior Manager, Trust and Safety, BIPL on the day when DPS MMS was put up for sale on Bazee.com. That is, the office responsible for the safety of the Portal, taking action on suspect lists when reported by our users, and block the user or close items listed accordingly. It was held that there is prima-facie sufficient material showing petitioners involvement to proceed against him for the commission of offence punishable under Section 292 IPC. Though he was already discharged of offences only under Section 67 read with Section 85 of IT Act and Section 294 IPC.

3. Dr. L. Prakash vs State Of Tamil Nadu (2002)

Petitioner was arrested by the Inspector of Police, R8 Vadapalani Police Station, Chennai for various offences, particularly Section 67 of the Information Technology Act, 2000, Section 4 read with Section 6 of the Indecent Representation of Women (Prohibition) Act, 1986 and Section 120-B of the Indian Penal Code.

4. Mohammed vs State on (2010)

Section 67 of Information Technology Act analyzed and held it is not applicable to the case of threatening email received by Chief Minster of Gujarat, hence ordered to be deleted from the matter.

Sec 67A - Publishing or Transmitting Sexually Explicit Act Electronically

Section 67A of Information Technology Act, 2000 amended by Information Technology (Amendment) Act, 2008is a species of cyber pornography defined in section 67 of the I.T. Act, 2000 specifically deal with publication and transmission of sexually explicit act or conduct of the person in the electronic form.

Sec 67A of Information Technology Act stands as :-

Whoever publishes or transmits or causes to be published or transmitted in the electronic form any material which contains sexually explicit act or conduct shall be punished on first conviction with imprisonment of either description for a term which may extend to five years and with fine which may extend to ten lakh rupees and in the event of second or subsequent conviction with imprisonment of either description for a term which may extend to seven years and also with fine which may extend to ten lakh rupees.

Publish simply means "to make public or make known to the public, to make generally accessible or available; to place before or offer to public; to bring before the public for sale or distribution."

Transmit means "to cause to be conveyed to another person or place; cause to pass on from one place or person to another; broadcast or send out; allow passing through a medium."

Electronic form means with reference to information means any information generated, sent, received or stored in media, magnetic, optical, computer memory, micro film, computer generated micro fiche or similar device.

The essential ingredients of this section are as follows:-

1.Publication or transmission or an act to be caused must be in electronic form.

2.Publication or transmission or an act to be caused must contains sexually explicit act in nature.

3.Publication or transmission or an act to be caused must contains sexually explicit conduct in nature.

Exception-

section 67A does not extend to any book, pamphlet, paper, writing, drawing, painting representation or figure in electronic form–

(*i*) the publication of which is proved to be justified as being for the public good on the ground that such book, pamphlet, paper, writing, drawing, painting representation or figure is the interest of science, literature, art or learning or other objects of general concern; or

(*ii*) which is kept or used for *bona fide* heritage or religious purposes.

The term 'sexually explicit act or conduct' has been qualified by the word 'explicit' meaning thereby that mere 'obscene act or conduct' may not fall under section 67 A.

The difference between Section 67 and 67A are:

1)Section 67 deals with punishment for publishing or transmitting obscenity in electric form, while Section 67A deals with punishment for publishing or transmitting sexually explicit act or conduct.

2)Section 67 is generic while Section 67A is specific.

3)The test of obscenity under Section 67 is likely audience test to prove obscenity where as the test of obscenity under Section 67A is 'no likely-audience test'.

4)The offence under Section 67 is bailable for first conviction and non-bailable for second or subsequent conviction while the offence under Section 67A is non-bailable for both first and second or subsequent convictions.

The offence has been penalised with imprisonment up to five years and fine up to ten lakhs or with both on first conviction and imprisonment up to seven years or fine up to ten lakhs or with both on second conviction. The offence is Non-bailable, cognizable and triable by the court of Judicial Magistrate First Class.

Sec 67B - Publishing or Transmitting Child Pornography Electronically

Section 67B of Information Technology Act, 2000 amended by Information Technology (Amendment) Act, 2008 is a species of cyber pornography defined in section 67 of the I.T. Act,

2000 specifically deal with publication and transmission of material depicting children in sexually explicit act in the electronic form. Simply this section deals with Child Pornography

Sec 67B of Information Technology Act stands as :-

Whoever,–

(*a*) publishes or transmits or causes to be published or transmitted material in any electronic form which depicts children engaged in sexually explicit act or conduct; or

(*b*) creates text or digital images, collects, seeks, browses, downloads, advertises, promotes, exchanges or distributes material in any electronic form depicting children in obscene or indecent or sexually explicit manner; or

(*c*) cultivates, entices or induces children to online relationship with one or more children for and on sexually explicit act or in a manner that may offend a reasonable adult on the computer resource; or

(*d*) facilitates abusing children online, or

(*e*) records in any electronic form own abuse or that of others pertaining to sexually explicit act with children,

shall be punished on first conviction with imprisonment of either description for a term which may extend to five years and with fine which may extend to ten lakh rupees and in the event of second or subsequent conviction with imprisonment of either description for a term which may extend to seven years and also with fine which may extend to ten lakh rupees:

Provided that provisions of section 67, section 67A and this section does not extend to any book, pamphlet, paper, writing, drawing, painting representation or figure in electronic form-

(i) the publication of which is proved to be justified as being for the public good on the ground that such book, pamphlet, paper, writing drawing, painting representation or figure is in the interest of science, literature, art or learning or other objects of general concern; or

(ii) which is kept or used for bona fide heritage or religious purposes.

Explanation– —children means a person who has not completed the age of 18 years.

Publish simply means "to make public or make known to the public, to make generally accessible or available; to place before or offer to public; to bring before the public for sale or distribution."

Transmit means "to cause to be conveyed to another person or place; cause to pass on from one place or person to another; broadcast or send out; allow passing through a medium."

Electronic form means with reference to information means any information generated, sent, received or stored in media, magnetic, optical, computer memory, micro film, computer generated micro fiche or similar device.

The essential ingredients of this sections are as follows:-

i) publishes or transmits or causes to be published or transmitted material in any electronic form;

ii). Publish or transmit material must depicts children engaged in sexually explicit act or conduct;

iii). It creates text or digital images, collects, seeks, browses, downloads, advertises, promotes, exchanges or distributes material in any electronic form depicting children in obscene or indecent or sexually explicit manner;

iv). cultivates, entices or induces children to online relationship with one or more children for and on sexually explicit act;

v) facilitates abusing children online;

vi) records in any electronic form own abuse or that of others pertaining to sexually explicit act with children,

The First conviction under Section 67B of the act was made on November 2009, when Lt. Col. Jagmohan Balbir Singh was arrested by the Cyber Cell of the Crime Branch police on the charge of uploading sexually explicit images and clips of children on child pornography websites. Lt. Col. Singh was charged under Section 67 B (punishment for publishing or transmitting of material depicting children in sexually explicit act, etc. in electronic form) of the Information Technology Act. It was the German police who first spotted the activity from Mumbai on a server located in the United States. They sent a report to the Interpol, which in turn forwarded it to the CBI Delhi, and subsequently to the Mumbai Crime Branch. The Cyber Cell tracked the server activity to the Internet Protocol (IP) address of Lt. Col Singh and subsequently he was arrested from his residence and charged with section 292 of IPC and 67B of IT Act 2000.

On 26th February 2016 the **Hon'ble Supreme Court** has ordered in the case of **Kamlesh Vaswani v. Union of India** of blocking of websites which contains sexually explicit material relates to child pornography. The order/direction reads as follows-

(a) To issue appropriate directions to Ministry of Communication and Information Technology -

(i) To take measures to promote the dissemination and improvement of filtering services.

(ii) To take strict measures to prevent distribution and access to pornography including measures regarding file sharing software.

(iii) To adopt various measures towardsimprovement in the effectiveness of blocking Child pornography on the Internet and to take measures to eliminate child pornography.

(b) To issue appropriate directions to Ministry of Women & Child Development

(i) For enhancement and to strengthening of protective measures to reinforce support for victims (both child and women).

(ii) To take effective steps to promote public relations and awareness raising activities concerning risks and proper use of the Internet.

(c) To issue appropriate directions to the Ministry of Human Resource Development

(i) To direct, that jammers be installed inside the school premises and in the school buses to prevent access of pornographic sites on the cell phones by the Driver or anyone who is in charge of the children in the Buses.

(ii) To direct, to have one male and female child counselor in every school and special workshop to be conducted in schools for awareness of sex education.

Exception-

section 67B does not extend to any book, pamphlet, paper, writing, drawing, painting representation or figure in electronic form–

(*i*) the publication of which is proved to be justified as being for the public good on the ground that such book, pamphlet, paper, writing, drawing, painting representation or figure is the interest of science, literature, art or learning or other objects of general concern; or

(*ii*) which is kept or used for *bona fide* heritage or religious purposes.

The Cybercafe should take adequate precautions to ensure computers installed at their facility are not used for law purposes.

The information Technology (Guidelines for Cyber Cafe) Rules, 2011 provides that:

(i)Cyber café shall take sufficient precautions to ensure that their computer resource are not utilised for any illegal activity (Rule 6(6)).

(ii)Cyber Cafe shall display a board clearly visible to the users, prohibiting them from viewing pornographic sites as well as copying or downloading information which is prohibited under the Law (Rule 6(7)).

(iii)Cyber cafe shall incorporate reasonable preventive measures to disallow the user from tampering with the computer system settings.

However, these measures will only prove effective if active supervision and monitoring of police or Registration authority appointed under the rules is maintained to ensure these provisions are effectively enforced and their licenses are revoked in case of defaults or violations.

The offence has been penalised with imprisonment up to five years and fine up to ten lakhs or with both on first conviction and imprisonment up to seven years or fine up to ten lakhs or with both on second conviction. The offence is Non-bailable, cognizable and triable by the court of Judicial Magistrate First Class.

Sec 67C – Preservation and Retention of Information

Section 67C of Information Technology Act, 2000 amended by Information Technology (Amendment) Act, 2008 specifically deal with preservation and retention of information by intermediaries.

Sec 67C of Information Technology Act stands as :-

(*1*) Intermediary shall preserve and retain such information as may be specified for such duration and in such manner and format as the Central Government may prescribe.

(*2*) any intermediary who intentionally or knowingly contravenes the provisions of sub section (*1*) shall be punished with an imprisonment for a term which may extend to three years and also be liable to fine.

The essential ingredients of this section are as follows:-

i). Intermediary has to preserve and retain the information for a duration;

ii). Intermediary have to preserve and retain the information in a manner

prescribed by the Central Government.

iii). Intermediary will be penalise under this section if knowingly or

intentionally failed to preserve and retain the information for a

duration and in a manner prescribed by the Central Government.

Sec 2 (i) (w) of the IT Act provides that 'intermediary', with respect to any particular electronic records, means any person who on behalf of another person receives, stores or transmits that record or provides any service with respect to that record and includes telecom service providers, network service providers, internet service providers, web-hosting service providers, search engines, online payment sites, online auction sites, online market places and cyber cafes.

The intermediary shall preserve and retain such information according to the prescription of the Central Government. The terms preservation and 'retention' are independent as one follows the other. It is preservation for retrieval. Preservation of information in electronic form is meant to be for effective, efficient and purposeful use. Registration is often seen as one of the means to preserve records, In order to preserve information, which exist in electronic form, Section 67C makes it mandatory to have backup files on backup media.

Section 67C shall be read with Section 7 if the IT Act, as the later lays down the conditions for the retention of electronic records, which are quite stringent in view of Section 7A, intermediaries may even be asked to have compulsory audit their preservation and retention policies.

Intermediaries shall have twin responsibilities i.e., to preserve and retain any information, as well as to implement and maintain reasonable security practices and procedures.

The offence is penalised with imprisonment up to three years or fine or with both Bailable and triable by the court of Judicial Magistrate First Class.

Sec 68- Power of Controller

According to section 68 of the Information Technology Act, the controller has a power to direct the Certifying Authority or any employee to take such measure or cease carrying on such activities as required for the compliance of the Act.

Sec 68 of Information Technology Act stands as:-

Power of Controller to give directions.–

(*1*) The Controller may, by order, direct a Certifying Authority or any employee of such Authority to take such measures or cease carrying on such activities as specified in the order if those are necessary to ensure compliance with the provisions of this Act, rules or any regulations made thereunder.

(*2*) Any person who intentionally or knowingly fails to comply with any order under sub section (*1*) shall be guilty of an offence and shall be liable on conviction to imprisonment for a term not exceeding two years or a fine not exceeding one lakh rupees or with both.

This section empowers the Controller to directL

(i)a Certifying Authority or any employee of such Authority

(ii)to take such measures or cease carrying on such activities

as specified in the order

(iii)the order should be passed only if necessary to ensure compliance with the provisions of Information Technology Act, rules or any regulations

It is clear from the wording of this section that the Controller could only give the directions to a Certifying Authority or any employee of such Authority

Controller has been defined under sec 2(*m*) of Information Technology Act 2000 as **"Controller means the Controller of Certifying Authorities appointed under sub-section (*1*) of section 17."**

Certifying Authority has been defined under sec 2(*g*)of Information Technology Act 2000 as **"Certifying Authority means a person who has been granted a licence to issue a electronic signature Certificate under section 24."**

The essential ingredients of this section are as follows:-

i). Controller may direct a certifying authority or employee of that authority to specified measures to comply with the provision of Information Technology Act.

ii). Controller may direct a certifying authority or employee of that authority to cease carrying to comply with the provision of Information Technology Act.

Furthermore, under Section 27 of the IT Act, the Controller has the power to delegate its authority to the Deputy Controller, Assistant Controller or any officer to exercise any of the powers of the controller under Chapter VI (Regulation of Certifying Authorities) of the Act. Hence, Section 68 may also be made applicable to the orders issued by Deputy Controller, Assistant Controller or any officer.

Section 28 and 25 of the IT Act extends the powers of the Controller to investigate contraventions involving certifying Authority or any employee of such Authority and may, by order, direct any person incharge of, or otherwise concerned with the operations of, the computer system, data, apparatus or any other material to provide reasonable technical and other assistance for the purpose of searching/obtaining any information or data contained in or available at such computer system (of Certifying Authority).

The offence has been penalised with imprisonment up to two years or fine up to one lakh or with both. The offence is bailable, cognizable and triable by the court of Judicial Magistrate First Class.

Sec 69- Interception, Monitoring or Decryption Of Any Information

Sec 69 is a very important section as it gives power to Cerntral and State Government to intercept, monitor or decrypt any information in the interest of the sovereignty or integrity of India, defence of India, security of the State, friendly relations with foreign States or public order or for preventing incitement to the commission of any cognizable offence.

Sec 69 of Information Technology Act stands as:-

Power to issue directions for interception or monitoring or decryption of any information through any computer resource.–

(*1*) Where the Central Government or a State Government or any of its officers specially authorised by the Central Government or the State Government, as the case may be, in this behalf may, if satisfied that it is necessary or expedient so to do, in the interest if the sovereignty or integrity of India, defence of India, security of the State, friendly relations with foreign States or public order or for preventing incitement to the commission of any cognizable offence relating to above or for investigation of any offence, it may subject to the provisions of sub-section (*2*), for reasons to be recorded in writing, by order, direct any agency of the appropriate Government to intercept, monitor or decrypt or cause to be intercepted or monitored or decrypted any information generated, transmitted, received or stored in any computer resource.

(*2*) The procedure and safeguards subject to which such interception or monitoring or decryption may be carried out, shall be such as may be prescribed.

(*3*) The subscriber or intermediary or any person in-charge of the computer resource shall, when called upon by any agency referred to in sub-section (*1*), extend all facilities and technical assistance to–

(*a*) provide access to or secure access to the computer resource generating, transmitting, receiving or storing such information; or

(*b*) intercept, monitor, or decrypt the information, as the case may be; or

(*c*) provide information stored in computer resource.

(*4*) The subscriber or intermediary or any person who fails to assist the agency referred to in sub-section (*3*) shall be punished with imprisonment for a term which may extend to seven years and shall also be liable to fine.

The essential ingredients of subsection of section 69 are as follows:

i). The central or state government can direct any of its officers or agency of the Government to intercept any information transmitted through any computer resource:

ii). The Central or State Government should have passed such direction on being satisfied that it is necessary or expedient to do so in the interest of the:-

a). sovereignty or integrity of India; or

b). the security of the state; or

c). friendly relations with foreign States; or

d). public order; or

e). for preventing incitement to the commission of any cognizable offence; or

f). for investigation of any offence.

iii). The reasons for such direction should be recorded in writing;

iv). The intermediary, subscriber or in-charge of the computer have to provide access to the computer resource;

v). The intermediary, subscriber or in-charge of the computer have to provide information stored in the computer resource;

vi). The intermediary, subscriber or in-charge if the computer have to assist the officer or agency in incepting, monitoring or decrypting any information.

The offence has been penalised with imprisonment up to seven years and fine. The offence is Non-bailable, cognizable and triable by the court of Judicial Magistrate First Class.

Sec 69A- Blocking of Public Access For Any Information

Sec 69A is a very important section as it gives power to Cerntral and State Government to block public access on any information in the interest of the sovereignty or integrity of India, defence of India, security of the State, friendly relations with foreign States or public order or for preventing incitement to the commission of any cognizable offence.

Sec 69A of Information Technology Act stands as:-

Power to issue directions for blocking for public access of any information through any computer resource.–

(*1*) Where the Central Government or any of its officers specially authorised by it in this behalf is satisfied that it is necessary or expedient so to do, in the interest of sovereignty and integrity of India, defence of India, security of the State, friendly relations with foreign States or public order or for preventing incitement to the commission of any cognizable offence relating to above, it may subject to the provisions of sub-section (*2*), for reasons to be recorded in writing, by order, direct any agency of the Government or intermediary to block for access by the public or cause to be blocked for access by the public any information generated, transmitted, received, stored or hosted in any computer resource.

(*2*) The procedure and safeguards subject to which such blocking for access by the public may be carried out, shall be such as may be prescribed.

(*3*) The intermediary who fails to comply with the direction issued under sub-section (*1*) shall be punished with an imprisonment for a term which may extend to seven years and also be liable to fine.

The essential ingredients of subsection of section 69A are as follows:

i). The central or state government can direct any of its officers or agency of the Government to block for access or cause to be block for access by public on any information in computer resource:

ii). Such information must be generated, transmitted, hosted, received or stored in a computer resource;

iii). The Central or State Government should have passed such direction on being satisfied that it is necessary or expedient to do so in the interest of the:-

a). sovereignty or integrity of India; or

b). the security of the state; or

c). friendly relations with forcign States; or

d). public order; or

e). for preventing incitement to the commission of any cognizable offence; or

iv). The reasons for such direction should be recorded in writing;

v). The intermediary, subscriber or in-charge of the computer have to provide access to the computer resource;

vi). The intermediary, subscriber or in-charge of the computer have to provide information stored in the computer resource;

vii). The intermediary, subscriber or in-charge if the computer have to assist the officer or agency in blocking for public access any information.

The offence has been penalised with imprisonment up to seven years and. The offence is Non-bailable, cognizable and triable by the court of Judicial Magistrate First Class.

<u>Sec 69B- Monitoring And Collecting of Data or Information For Cyber Security</u>

Sec 69B is a very important section as it gives power to Cerntral Government to monitor and collect traffic data or information in any computer resource to enhance the Cyber Security and for identification, analysis and prevention of introducing or spreading of computer contaminant in the Nation.

Sec 69B of Information Technology Act stands as:-

Power to authorise to monitor and collect traffic data or information through any computer resource for cyber security.–

(*1*) The Central Government may, to enhance cyber security and for identification, analysis and prevention of intrusion or spread of computer contaminant in the country, by notification in the Official Gazette, authorise any agency of the Government to monitor and collect traffic data or information generated, transmitted, received or stored in any computer resource.

(*2*) The intermediary or any person in-charge or the computer resource shall, when called upon by the agency which has been authorised under sub-section (*1*), provide technical assistance and extend all facilities to such agency to enable online access or to secure and provide online access to the computer resource generating, transmitting, receiving or storing such traffic data or information.

(*3*) The procedure and safeguards for monitoring and collecting traffic data or information, shall be such as may be prescribed.

(*4*) Any intermediary who intentionally or knowingly contravenes the provisions of sub section (*2*) shall be punished with an imprisonment for a term which any extend to three years and shall also be liable to fine.

Explanation.–For the purposes of this section,–

(*i*) —computer contaminant shall have the meaning assigned to it in section 43;

(*ii*) —traffic data means any data identifying or purporting to identify any person, computer system or computer network or location to or from which the communication is or may be transmitted and includes communications origin, destination, route, time, data, size, duration or type of underlying service and any other information.

The Central Government may authorize any agency of the Government to monitor and collect traffic data or information generated, transmitted, received or stored in any computer resource for the following reasons:

(i)to enhance Cyber Security and for identification,

(ii)analysis and prevention of any intrusion or spread of computer contaminant in the country.

The essential ingredients of subsection of section 69B are as follows:

i). The Central Government can direct any of its officers or agency of the Government to monitor and collect traffic data or information in computer resource:

ii). Such information must be generated, transmitted, received or stored in a computer resource;

iii). The Central Government should have made such authorisation to enhance the Cyber Security in the Nation;

iv). Such authorisation must be made by published notification in official Gazette;

v). That Such authorisation has been given on account for identification, analysis and prevention of intrusion in country;

vi). v). That Such authorisation has been given on account for identification, analysis and prevention of spread of computer contaminant in country;

vii). The intermediary, subscriber or in-charge if the computer have to assist the officer or agency in blocking for public access any information.

viii). The procedure of monitoring and collecting of traffic data and information must be prescribed.

The offence has been penalised with imprisonment up to three years and fine. The offence is bailable, cognizable and triable by the court of Judicial Magistrate First Class.

<u>Sec 70- Protected System</u>

Section 70 of the Information Technology Act empowers the appropriate government to declare any computer, computer system or computer network to be a protected system, by notification in the official gazette.

Sec 70 of Information Technology Act stands as:-

Protected system.–

(*1*) The appropriate Government may, by notification in the Official Gazette, declare any computer resource which directly or indirectly affects the facility of Critical Information Infrastructure, to be a protected system.

Explanation.–For the purposes of this section, —

Critical Information Infrastructure means the computer resource, the incapacitation or destruction of which, shall have debilitating impact on national security, economy, public health or safety.

(*2*) The appropriate Government may, by order in writing, authorise the person who are authorised to access protected systems notified under sub-section (*1*).

(*3*) Any person who secures access or attempts to secure access to a protected system in contravention of the provisions of this section shall be punished with imprisonment of either description for a term which may extend to ten years and shall also be liable to fine.

(*4*) The Central Government shall prescribe the information security practices and procedures for such protected system.

The appropriate government has to issue by notification in the Official Gazette declaring any computer resource which directly or indirectly affects the facility of Critical Information Infrastructure as a protected system.

The Central Government is empowered by this Section to authorize the person who are authorized to access such protected system by order in writing.

Illustration:If the computer network of the Indian Army is to be declared as a protected system, the Central Government would be the appropriate Government and If the computer network of the Indore Police is to be declared as a protected system, the Government of Madhya Pradesh would be the appropriate Government but If the computer network of the Forest Department in Madhya Pradesh is to be declared as a protected system, the Central Government and Government of Madhya Pradesh would be the appropriate Government.

Illustration:Chetan runs a password cracking software to crack the password of a protected system. Irrespective of whether he succeeds in cracking the password, he is guilty of attempting to secure access.

The essential ingredients of this section are as follows:-

i). The appropriate Government should have declared any computer, computer system or computer network to be a protected system;

ii). The notification may be published in the Official Gazette as well as in the electronic gazette within the meaning of section 8 of the Information Technology Act, 2000.

iii). Secured access or attempted to secure access to the notified protected system must be made;

iv). The information must be critical;

v). Access to the critical information may lead effect on

a). National Security; or

b). National Economy; or

c). Public Health; or

d). Public Safety.

vi). The appropriate government must authorise person in writing to access the protected system;

vii). Offender must be access without authorisation.

The offence has been penalised with imprisonment up to ten years and fine. The offence is Non-bailable, cognizable and triable by the Session court.

Sec 70B- Indian Computer Emergency Response Team

Sec 70B is an important section in Information Technology Act as Section 70B is dedicated to the Indian Computer Emergency Response Team (I-CERT) as also its functions, duties and connected issues and offences. Section 70B states that the Indian Computer Emergency Response Team to serve as the national agency for incident response.

Sec 70B of Information Technology Act stands as:-

Indian Computer Emergency Response Team to serve as national agency for incident response.–

(*1*) The Central Government shall, by notification in the Official Gazette, appoint an agency of the Government to be called the Indian Computer Emergency Response Team.

(*2*) The Central Government shall provide the agency referred to in sub-section (*1*) with a Director General and such other officers and employees as may be prescribed.

(*3*) The salary and allowances and terms and conditions of the Director-General and other officers and employees shall be such as may be prescribed.

(*4*) The Indian Computer Emergency Response Team shall serve as the national agency for performing the following functions in the area of cyber security,–

(*a*) collection, analysis and dissemination of information on cyber incidents;

(*b*) forecast and alerts of cyber security incidents;

(*c*) emergency measures for handling cyber security incidents;

(*d*) coordination of cyber incidents response activities;

(*e*) issue guidelines, advisories, vulnerability notes and white papers relating to information security practices, procedures, preventation, response and reporting of cyber incidents;

(*f*) such other functions relating to cyber security as may be prescribed.

(*5*) The manner of performing functions and duties of the agency referred to in sub section (*1*) shall be such as may be prescribed.

(*6*) For carrying out the provisions of sub-section (*4*), the agency referred to in sub section (*1*) may call for information and give direction to the service providers, intermediaries, data centres, body corporate and any other person.

(*7*) Any service provider, intermediaries, data centers, body corporate or person who fails to provide the information called for or comply with the direction under sub-section (*6*), shall be punishable with imprisonment for a term which may extend to one year or with fine which may extend to one lakh rupees or with both.

(*8*) No court shall take cognizance of any offence under this section, except on a complaint made by an officer authorised in this behalf by the agency referred to in sub section (*1*).

The essential ingredients of this section are as follows:-

i). The appointment of a Government Agency must be published in a Official Gazette;

ii). The agency appointed as Indian Computer Emergency Response Team must be worked in the area of Cyber Security;

iii). Service Provider, intermediaries, data centers, body corporate or person fails to comply with the direction of the Indian Computer Emergency Response Team;

iv). Service Provider, intermediaries, data centers, body corporate or person fails to provide information called by the Indian Computer Emergency Response Team;

v). The Court can take cognizance only on a complaint made by the officer authorised by the agency.

The offence has been penalised with imprisonment up to one years or fine up to one lakh or with both. The offence is bailable, Non-cognizable and triable by the court of Judicial Magistrate First Class.

Sec 71- Penalty For Misrepresentation

Sec 71 of information Technology Act deals with the person obtains the license or electronic signature by misrepresenting him or suppressing any fact from the Controller or Certifying Authority

Sec 71 of Information Technology Act stands as :-

Penalty for misrepresentation.–

Whoever makes any misrepresentation to, or suppresses any material fact from the Controller or the Certifying Authority for obtaining any licence or electronic signature Certificate, as the case may be, shall be punished with imprisonment for a term which may extend to two years, or with fine which may extend to one lakh rupees, or with both.

Certifying Authority means a person who has been granted a license to issue Digital Signature Certificate Under section 24.

Controller' means the Controller of Certifying Authority appointed under sub section (1) of sec 17.

Misrepresentation means to submit false or incorrect facts

Suppression means to non-disclosure of the information

When a person applies for a electronic signature certificate has to fill a form with all necessary information as prescribed by Rule 23 of the Information Technology (Certifying Authorities) Rules, 2000 and as provided in Schedule IV of the said rules.

While applying for a license, a person is required to fill a form with all necessary information as prescribed by Rule 10 of the Information Technology (Certifying Authorities) Rules, 2000 and as provided in Schedule I of the said rules.

The essential ingredients of this section are as follows:-

1. The person had made misrepresentation to the controller or certifying authority.
2. The person had suppress the material facts from the controller or certifying authority.
3. The act has been done to obtain the license or electronic signature.

Illustration- Chetan applied to obtain license for certifying authority. Chetan fills his name as Ashish in the form and attached the copies of Ashish documents. Chetan is liable under this section.

The offence has been penalised with imprisonment up to two years or fine up to one lakh or with both. The offence is bailable, Non-cognizable and triable by the court of Judicial Magistrate First Class.

Sec 72- Breach of Confidentiality and Privacy

Right to privacy, in India, has been held to be covered under the ambit of Article 21 of the Constitution of India and Sec 72 deals with the safeguarding and penalizing from breaching the privacy and confidentiality electronically.

Sec 72 of Information Technology Act stands as:-

Penalty for Breach of confidentiality and privacy.–

Save as otherwise provided in this Act or any other law for the time being in force, if any person who, in pursuance of any of the powers conferred under this Act, rules or regulations made there under, has secured access to any electronic record, book, register, correspondence, information, document or other material without the consent of the person concerned discloses such electronic record, book, register, correspondence, information, document or other material to any other person shall be punished with imprisonment for a term which may extend to two years, or with fine which may extend to one lakh rupees, or with both.

The essential ingredients of this section are as follows:-

1. A person disclosed the electronic record, book, register, correspondence, information, document or any other material to third person.

2. The person had secured access to the electronic record, book, register, correspondence, information, document or other material in pursuance of the powers this act, rules or regulations made;

3. The electronic records etc. should have been disclosed without the consent of person.

The Idea behind Section 72 of IT Act is that the person who has secured to any such information shall not take unfair advantage of it by disclosing it to the third party without obtaining the Consent of the disclosing party. An obligation of confidence arises between the 'data collectors', 'data controller' and a 'data subject'.

Illustration- Ashish is a Inspector a investigating an offence covers under the IT Act. Ashish seize various electronic material from suspect Chetan contains evidence. Ashish shows the evidence to the press without obtaining consent from Chetan. Ashish is liable under this section.

Illustration- Chetan being an Assistant Superintendent of Police raids at Ashish house investigating the offence covered under IT Act. Chetan seized various kind of electronic evidence in form of CD, pen drive, Hard disk etc., Chetan submits and disclose the information in the court without obtaining consent from Ashish. Chetan is not liable under this Section.

The offence has been penalised with imprisonment up to two years or fine up to one lakh or with both. The offence is bailable, Non-cognizable and triable by the court of Judicial Magistrate First Class.

<u>Sec 72A- Breach of Lawful Contract</u>

Sec 72A deals with the punishment for breach of lawful contract for disclosure of Information.

Sec 72A of Information Technology Act stands as:-

Punishment for disclosure of information in breach of lawful contract.–

Save as otherwise provided in this Act or any other law for the time being in force, any person including an intermediary who, while providing services under the terms of lawful contract, has secured access to any material containing personal information about another person, with the intent to cause or knowing that he is likely to cause wrongful loss or wrongful gain discloses, without the consent of the person concerned, or in breach of a lawful contract, such material to any other person, shall be punished with imprisonment for a term which may extend to three years, or with fine which may extend to five lakh rupees, or with both.

Section 72A creates a liabilities for service providers, including an intermediary. It is kind of data protection measure, wherein a service provider who has secured access to any material containing personal information about a person, disclose such information without the consent of the person concerned or in breach of lawful contract, with the internet to cause or knowing that he is likely to cause wrongful loss or wrongful gain to such a person.

The essential ingredients of this section are as follows:-

i). Any person including intermediary providing service under the lawful contract secured access any material containing personal information of another person;

ii).Any person including intermediary discloses personal information of third person without his/her consent;

iii). Act has been done intent or knowing to cause wrongful loss or wrongful gain to third person;

Illustration: Chetan is working in a multinational company as data operator. Ashish who is the owner of rivalry company offers bribe Chetan to handover the clients data. Chetan provided the clients data of his company for wrongful gain. Chetan has disclose the information in breach of contract. Chetan is liable under this section.

Illsutration:- Ashish is working in a mobile network company as operator and authorise to access the records of the customer. Chetan who is a police inspector class the call details and data of a suspected person in a offence who is also the customer of his mobile network company. Ashish provides the data to Chetan. Ashish is not liable under this section as he is assisting the police and work under the law.

The offence has been penalised with imprisonment up to three years or fine up to five lakhs or with both. The offence is bailable, cognizable and triable by the court of Judicial Magistrate First Class.

<u>Sec 73- False Electronic Signature Certificate</u>

Section 73 makes publishing of an Electronic Signature Certificate, which is false in certain particulars, a penal offence. This section is basically enacted to prevent false Electronic Signature Certificates from being published for pecuniary gain or criminal purposes.

Sec 73 of Information Technology Act stands as:-

Penalty for publishing electronic signature Certificate false in certain particulars.–

(*1*) No person shall publish a electronic signature Certificate or otherwise make it available to any other person with the knowledge that–

(*a*) the Certifying Authority listed in the certificate has not issued it; or

(*b*) the subscriber listed in the certificate has not accepted it; or

(*c*) the certificate has been revoked or suspended, unless such publication is for the purpose of verifying a electronic signature created prior to such suspension or revocation.

(*2*) Any person who contravenes the provisions of sub-section (*1*) shall be punished with imprisonment for a term which may extend to two years, or with fine which may extend to one lakh rupees, or with both.

The **Hon'ble Supreme Court** defined the term 'publication' in the case of ***Bennett Coleman & Co. v. Union of India***. The term 'publication' means dissemination and circulation. The term includes dissemination, storage and transmission of information or data in electronic form if we talk about in the context of digital medium.

The essential ingredients of this section are as follows:-

i). Person publish a Electronic Signature Certificate;

ii). Person makes available to third person;

iii). Person done the act has knowledge that the electronic signature certificate has not been issued by certifying authority;

iv). Person done the act has knowledge that the subscriber list in the electronic signature certificate has not accepted it;

v). Person done the act has knowledge that the electronic signature certificate has been suspended or revoked;

vi). There is no offence if the act has been done having purpose of verifying a created electronic signature prior to the suspension or revocation.

Illustration:- Ashish had made false electronic signature certificate by a certifying authority and post it in his website. Ashish by using that certificate committed fraud. Ashish is liable under this section.

Illustration:- Chetan is the owner of the company in which Ashish is working. Ashish has obtained a electronic signature certificate but it has been suspended after he shift his job. Chetan provides that electronic signature to sandeep to verify the documents and work done by Ashish before shifting of his job. Chetan is not liable under this section.

The offence has been penalised with imprisonment up to two years or fine up to one lakh or with both. The offence is bailable, Non-cognizable and triable by the court of Judicial Magistrate First Class.

Sec 74- Publication For Fraudulent Purpose

Section 74 creates a distinct kind of crime, which deals with publication of Electronic/ Digital Signatures for fraudulent purposes

Sec 74 of Information Technology Act stands as:-

Publication for fraudulent purpose.–

Whoever knowingly creates, publishes or otherwise makes available a electronic signature Certificate for any fraudulent or unlawful purpose shall be punished with imprisonment for a term which may extend to two years, or with fine which may extend to one lakh rupees, or with both.

The **Hon'ble Supreme Court** defined the term 'publication' in the case of ***Bennett Coleman & Co. v. Union of India.*** The term 'publication' means dissemination and circulation. The term includes dissemination, storage and transmission of information or data in electronic form if we talk about in the context of digital medium.

In Section 74 of the IT Act, 2000, the onus is on both the Certifying Authority and subscriber to create, publish or otherwise make available an electronic signature certificate for any fraudulent or unlawful purpose.

The essential ingredients of this section are as follows:-

i). Person creates or publish a Electronic Signature Certificate;

ii). Person makes available to third person;

iii). Person done the act has knowledge that the electronic signature certificate has been used for fraudulently purpose.

iv). Person done the act has knowledge that the electronic signature certificate has been used for unlawful purpose.

Illustration:- Ashish had creates a false electronic signature certificate by a certifying authority and post it in his website. Ashish by using that certificate committed fraud. Ashish is liable under this section.

Illustration:- Chetan made available a electronic signature certificate by a certifying authority to Ashish having knowledge that Ashish will use the certificate unlawfully. Ashish by using that certificate committed unlawful Act. Chetan is liable under this section.

The offence has been penalised with imprisonment up to two years or fine up to one lakh or with both. The offence is bailable, Non-cognizable and triable by the court of Judicial Magistrate First Class.

Sec 85- Offence By Companies

Section 85 of the Information Technology Act incorporates the concept of corporate criminal liability, or the criminal liability imposed on a company for its contravention of the Act or any rule, direction or order made there under. The explanation to this section provides that a company is anybody corporate, including a firm or association of individuals. The company may be corporate or incorporated.

Sec 85 of Information Technology stands as:-

Offences by companies.–

(*1*) Where a person committing a contravention of any of the provisions of this Act or of any rule, direction or order made thereunder is a company, every person who, at the time the contravention was committed, was in charge of, and was responsible to, the company for the conduct of business of the company as well as the company, shall be guilty of the contravention and shall be liable to be proceeded against and punished accordingly:

Provided that nothing contained in this sub-section shall render any such person liable to punishment if he proves that the contravention took place without his knowledge or that he exercised all due diligence to prevent such contravention.

(*2*) Notwithstanding anything contained in sub-section (*1*), where a contravention of any of the provisions of this Act or of any rule, direction or order made thereunder has been committed by a company and it is proved that the contravention has taken place with the consent or connivance of, or is attributable to any neglect on the part of, any director, manager, secretary or other officer of the company, such director, manager, secretary or other officer shall also be deemed to be guilty of the contravention and shall be liable to be proceeded against and punished accordingly.

Explanation.–For the purposes of this section,–

(*i*) —company means any body corporate and includes a firm or other association of individuals; and

(*ii*) —director, in relation to a firm, means a partner in the firm.

The said section provides that if a person committing a contravention of any of the provisions of this Act or any rule, direction or order made there under is a company, every person who was in charge of and was responsible to the company for the conduct of business of the company as well as the company at the time the contravention was committed, shall be liable to punishment.

III. Indian Penal Code, 1860 (Amendment)

After the introduction of Information Technology Act 2000 and in absence of any provision relating to offence and punishment it was necessary to amend the Indian Penal Act to deal with the punishments relating to cyber crimes. In relation to cyber crime there are many sections which were substituted so some are newly inserted. The following sections are as follows:-

Section 29 – Electronic Record

"29A. The words "electronic record" shall have the meaning assigned to them in clause (t) of sub-section (1) of section 2 of the Information Technology Act, 2000".

Section 167 - Public servant framing an incorrect document with intent to cause injury .

In this Section words **"such public servant, charged with the preparation or translation of any document, frames or translates that document"**, has been substituted to **"such public servant, charged with the preparation or translation of any document or electronic record, frames, prepares or translates that document or electronic record"**

Section 172 -Absconding to avoid service of summons of other proceeding.

In this section words **"produce a document in a Court of Justice"** has been substituted to **"produce a document or an electronic record in a Court of Justice"**

Section 173,- Preventing service of summons or other proceeding, or preventing publication thereof.

In this section words **"to produce a document in Court of Justice"** has been substituted to **"to produce a document or electronic record in a Court of Justice"**

section 175 -Omission to produce document to public servant by person legal ly bound to produce it.

In this section words **"document"** where it occurs has been substituted to **"document or electronic record"**.

Section 192 – Fabricating False Evidence

In this section words **"makes any false entry in any book or record, or makes any document containing a false statement"** has been substituted to **"makes any false entry in any book or record, or electronic record or makes any document or electronic record containing a false statement5'**.

Section 204 – Destruction of Documents or Electronic Record to prevent its production as evidence

In this Section word **"document"** at where it occurs, has been substituted to **"document or electronic record"**.

Section 463 -Forgery

In this section words **"Whoever makes any false documents or part of a document with intent to cause damage or injury"** has been substituted to **"Whoever makes any false documents or false electronic record or part of a document or electronic record, with intent to cause damage or injury"**.

Section 464 – Making A False Document

In this Section From the begining **"A person is said to make a false document"** to the ending **"by reason of deception practiced upon him, he does not know the contents of the document or the nature of the alteration"**, the following substitution has been done:

"A person is said to make a false document or false electronic record:

"First, who dishonestly or fraudulently:

a) makes, signs, seals or executes a document or part of a document;

b) makes or transmits any electronic record or part of any electronic record;

c) affixes any digital signature on any electronic record;

d) makes any mark denoting the execution of a document or

the authenticity of the digital signature, with the intention of causing it to be believed that such document or part of document, electronic record or digital signature was made, signed, sealed, executed, transmitted or affixed by or by the authority of a person by whom or by whose authority he knows that it was not made, signed, sealed, executed or affixed; or

"Second, who, without lawful authority, dishonestly or fraudulently, by cancellation or otherwise, alters a document or an electronic record in any material part thereof, after it has been made, executed or affixed with digital signature either by himself or by any other person, whether such person be living or dead at the time of such alteration; or

"Third, who dishonestly or fraudulently causes any person to sign, seal, execute or alter a document or an electronic record or to affix his digital signature on any electronic record knowing that such person by reason ofunsoundness of mind or intoxication cannot, or that by reason ofdeception Dracticed upon him, he does not know the contents of the document or electronic record or the nature of the alteration."

Explanation 3 has been inserted after explanation 2 at the end as

Explanation 3: For the purposes of this section, the expression "affixing digital signature" shall have the meaning assigned to it in clause (d) of subsection (1) of section 2 of the Information .Technology Act, 2000.

Section 466 – Forgery of record of court or of public register etc.

In this section words **"Whoever forges a document"** has been substituted to **"Whoever forges a document or an electronic record"**;

and explanation shall be inserted at the end, namely:

Explanation: For the purposes of this section, "register" includes any list, data or record of any entries maintained in the electronic form as defined in clause of sub-section (1) of section 2 of the Information Technology Act, 2000".

Section 468 – Forgery For Purpose of Cheating

In this Section words **"document forged"**, has been substituted to **"document or electronic record forged"**.

Section 469 – Forgery For Purpose of Harming Reputation

In this section words **"intending that the document forged"** has been substituted to **"intending that the document or electronic record forged"**.

Section 470 – Forged Document or Electronic Record

In this section word **"document"** where it occurs has been substituted to **"document or electronic record"**.

Section 471 – Using as Genuine a Forged Document or Electronic Record

In this section word **"document"** wherever it occurs, has been substituted to **"document or electronic record"**.

Section 474 – Having possession of document described in section 466 or 467, knowing it to be forged and intending to use it as genuine.

This section has been completely substituted as follows:-

"Whoever has in his possession any document or electronic record, knowing the same to be forged and intending that the same shall fraudulently or dishonestly be used as a genuine, shall, if the document or electronic record is one of the description mentioned in section 466 of this Code".

Section 476 – Counterfeiting device or mark used for authenticating documents other than those described in section 467, or possessing counterfeit marked material.

In this section words **"any document"**, has been substituted to **"any document or electronic record"**.

Section 477A – Falsification of Documents

In this Section words **"book, paper, writing"** where they occurs has been substituted to **"book, electronic record, paper, writing"**.

IV. INDIAN EVIDENCE ACT, 1872 (Amendement)

After the introduction of Information Technology Act 2000 and in absence of any provision relating to evidence it was necessary to amend the Indian Evidence Act, 1872 to deal with the acceptance of evidence relating to cyber crimes. In relation to cyber crime there are many sections which were substituted so some are newly inserted. The following sections are as follows:-

Section 3 – Interpretation Clause

i) In the definition of **"Evidence"** words **"all documents produced for the inspection of the Court"** has been substituted to **"all documents including electronic records produced for the inspection of the Court"**;

ii) After the definition of "India", the following shall be inserted, namely: 'the expressions "Certifying Authority", "digital signature", "Digital Signature Certificate", "electronic form", "electronic records", "information", "secure electronic record", "secure digital signature" and "subscriber" shall have the meanings respectively assigned to them in the Information Technology Act, 2000.

Section 17 – Admission Defined

In this Section words **"oral or documentary,"** has been substituted to **"oral or documentary or contained in electronic form"**.

Section 22A -When oral admission as to contents of electronic records are relevant.

A new Section 22A has been inserted after section 22 as:-

"22A. Oral admissions as to the contents of electronic records are not relevant, unless the genuineness of the electronic record produced is in question".

Section 34- Entries in the books of account, including those maintained

in an electronic form

In this section words **"Entries in the books of account"** has been substituted to **"Entries in the books of account, including those maintained in an electronic form"**.

Section 35 – Relevancy of Entry in Public Record or an Electronic Record

In this Section word **"record"** where it occurs has been substituted to **"record or an electronic record"**.

Section 39- What evidence to be given when statement forms part of a conversation, document, electronic record, book or series of letters or papers.

In this section the whole section has been substituted to new section as:-

"39. When any statement of which evidence is given forms part of a longer statement, or of a conversation or pan of an isolated document, or is contained in a document which forms part of a book, or is contained in part of electronic record or of a connected series of letters or papers, evidence shall be given of so much and no more of the statement, conversation, document, electronic record, book or series of letters or papers as the Court considers necessary in that particular case to the full understanding of the nature and effect of the statement, and of the circumstances under which it was made".

Section 47A. Opinion as to digital signature where relevant.

A new Section 47A has been inserted after section 47 as:-

"47A. When the Court has 10 form an opinion as to the digital signature of any person, the opinion of the Certifying Authority which has issued the Digital Signature Certificate is a relevant fact".

Section 59 – Proof Of Facts By Oral Evidence

In this section words **"contents of documents"** has been substituted to **"contents of documents or electronic records"**.

Section 65A. Special provisions as to evidence relating to electronic record

A new Section 65A has been inserted after section 65 as:-

"65A. The contents of electronic records may be proved in accordance with the provisions of section 65B."

Section 65B -Admissibility of electronic records

A new Section 65B has been inserted after section 65A as:-

" (1) Notwithstanding anything contained in this Act, any information contained in an electronic record which is printed on a paper, stored, recorded or copied in optical or magnetic media produced by a computer (hereinafter referred to as the computer output) shall be deemed to be also a document, if the conditions mentioned in this section are satisfied in relation to the information and computer in question and shall be admissible in any proceedings, without further proof or production of the original, as evidence of any contents of the original or of any fact stated therein of which direct evidence would be admissible.

2) The conditions referred to in sub-section (1) in respect of a computer output shall be the following, namely:

a) the computer output containing the information was produced by the computer during the period over which the computer was used regularly to store or process information for the purposes of any activities regularly carried on over that period by the person having lawful control over the use of the computer;

b) during the said period, information of the kind contained in the electronic record or of the kind from which the information so contained is derived was regularly fed into the computer in the ordinary course of the said activities;

c) throughout the material part of the said period, the computer was operating properly or, if not, then in respect of any period in which it was not operating properly or was out of operation during that part of the period, was not such as to affect the electronic record or the accuracy of its contents; and

d) the information contained in the electronic record reproduces or is derived from such information fed into the computer in the ordinary course of the said activities.

3) Where over any period, the function of storing or processing information for the purposes of any activities regularly carried on over that period as mentioned in clause (a) of sub-section (2) was regularly performed by computers, whether:

a) by a combination of computers operating over that period; or

b) by different computers operating in succession over that period; or

c) by different combinations of computers operating in succession over that period; or

d) in any other manner involving the successive operation over that period, in whatever order, of one or more computers and one or more combinations of computers, all the computers used for that purpose during that period shall be treated for the purposes of this section as constituting a single computer; and references in this section to a computer shall be construed accordingly.

4) In any proceedings where it is desired to give a statement in evidence by virtue of this section, a certificate doing any of the following things, that is to say,

a) identifying the electronic record containing the statement and describing the manner in which it was produced;

b) giving such particulars of any device involved in the production of that electronic record as may be appropriate for the purpose of showing that the electronic record was produced by a computer;

c) dealing with any of the matters to which the conditions mentioned in sub section (2) relate, and purporting to be signed by a person occupying a responsible official position in relation to the operation of the relevant device or the management of the relevant activities (whichever is appropriate) shall be evidence of any matter stated in the certificate; and for the purposes of this sub-section it shall be sufficient for a matter to be stated to the best of the knowledge and belief of the person stating it

5) For the purposes of this section,

a) information shall be taken to be supplied to a computer if it is supplied thereto in any appropriate form and whether it is so supplied directly or (with or without human intervention) by means of any appropriate equipment;

b) whether in the course, of activities carried on by any official, information is supplied with a view to its being stored or processed for the purposes of those activities by a computer operated otherwise than in the course of those activities, that information, if duly supplied to that computer, shall be taken to be supplied to it in the course of those activities;

c) a computer output shall be taken to have been produced by a computer whether it was produced by it directly or (with or without human intervention) by means of any appropriate equipment.

Explanation: For the purposes of this section any reference to information being derived from other information shall be a reference to its being derived there from by calculation, comparison or any other process.

Section 67A - Proof as to digital signature

A new Section 67A has been inserted after section 67 as:-

"67A. Except in the case of a secure digital signature, if the digital signature of any subscriber is alleged to have been affixed to an electronic record the fact that such digital signature is the digital signature of the subscriber must be proved."

Section 73A- Proof as to verification of digital signature

A new Section 73A has been inserted after section 73 as:-

"73 A. In order to ascertain whether a digital signature is that of the person by whom it purports to have been affixed, the Court may direct

a) that person or the Controller or the Certifying Authority to produce the Digital Signature Certificate;

b) any other person to apply the public key listed in the Digital Signature Certificate and verify the digital signature purported to have been affixed by that person.

Explanation: For the purposes of this section, "Controller" means the Controller appointed under sub-section (1) of section 17 of the Information Technology Act, 2000'.

Section 81A Presumption as to Gazettes in electronic forms

A new Section 81A has been inserted after section 81 as:-

"81 A. The Court shall presume the genuineness of every electronic record purporting to be the Official Gazette, or purporting to be electronic record directed by any law to be kept by any person, if such electronic record is kept substantially in the form required by law and is produced from proper custody".

Section 85A - Presumption as to electronic agreements.

A new Section 85A has been inserted after section 85 as:-

"85A. The Court shall presume that eveiy electronic record purporting to be an agreement containing the digital signatures of the parties was so concluded by affixing the digital signature of the parties".

Section 85B -Presumption as to electronic records and digital signatures

A new Section 85B has been inserted after section 85 as:-

"85B. (1) In any proceedings involving a secure electronic record, the Court shall presume unless contrary is proved, that the secure electronic record has not been altered since the specific point of time to which the secure status relates.

2) In any proceedings, involving secure digital signature, the Court shall presume unless the contrary is proved that:

a) the secure digital signature is affixed by subscriber with the intention of signing or approving the electronic record;

b) except in the case of a secure electronic record or a secure digital signature, nothing in this section shall create any presumption relating to authenticity and integrity of the electronic record or any digital signature.

Section 85C -Presumption as to digital signature certificates

A new Section 85C has been inserted after section 85 as:-

"85C.The Court shall presume, unless contrary is proved, that the information listed in a Digital Signature Certificate is correct, except for information specified as subscriber information which has not been verified, if the certificate was accepted by the subscriber".

Section 88A - Presumption as to electronic messages

A new Section 88A has been inserted after section 88 as:-

88A. The Court may presume that an electronic message forwarded by the originator through an electronic mail server to the addressee to whom the message purports to be addressed corresponds with the message as fed into his computer for transmission; but the Court shall not make any presumption as to the person by whom such message was sent.

Explanation: For the purposes of this section, the expressions "addressee" and "originator" shall have the same meanings respectively assigned to them in clauses (b) and (za) of sub-section (1) of section 2 of the Information Technology Act, 2000.

Section 90A - Presumption as to electronic records five years old.

A new Section 90A has been inserted after section 90 as:-

"90A. Where any electronic record, purporting or proved to be five years old, is produced from any custody which the Court in the particular case considers proper, the Court may presume that the digital signature which puiports to be the digital signature of any particular person was so affixed by him or any person authorised by him in this behalf.

Explanation: Electronic records are said to be in proper custody if they are in the place in which, and under the care of the person with whom, they naturally be; but no custody is improper if it is proved to have had a legitimate origin, or the circumstances of the particular case are such as to render such an origin probable.

This Explanation applies also to section 81 A".

Section 131- Production of documents or electronic records which another person, having possession, could refuse to produce.

In this section the whole section has been substituted to new section as:-

"131. No one shall be compelled to produce documents in his possession or electronic records under his control, which any other person would be entitled to refuse to produce if they were in his possession or control, unless such last mentioned person consents to then production".

V. BANKERS' BOOKS EVIDENCE ACT 1891 (Amendment)

After the introduction of Information Technology Act 2000 and in absence of any provision relating to evidence it was necessary to amend the Banker's Book Amendment act to deal with the offences relating to cyber crimes. In relation to cyber crime there are many sections which were substituted so some are newly inserted. The following sections are as follows:-

section 2 – Definitions

In clause (3), the clause has been substituted as:

(3) "bankers' books" include ledgers, day-books, cash- books, account-books and all other books used in the ordinary business of a bank whether kept in the written form or as printouts of data stored in a floppy, disc, tape or any other form of electromagnetic data storage device;

In clause (8), the clause has been substituted as:

(8) "certified copy" means when the books of a bank:

a) are maintained in written form, a copy of any entry in such books together with a certificate written; the foot of such copy that it is a true copy of such entry, that such entry is contained in one of the ordinary books of the bank and was made in the usual and ordinary course of business and that such book is still in the custody of the bank, and where the copy was obtained by a mechanical or other process which in itself ensured the accuracy of the copy, a further certificate to that effect, but where the book from which such copy was prepared has been destroyed in the usual course of the bank's business after the date on which the copy had been so prepared, a further certificate to that effect, each such certificate being dated and subscribed by the principal accountant or manager of the bank with his name and official tide; and

b) consist of printouts of data stored in a floppy, disc, tape or any other electromagnetic data storage device, a printout of such entry or a copy of such printout together with such statements certified in accordance with die provisions of section 2A.

Section 2A –Conditions in the printout.

A new Section 2A has been inserted after section 2 as:-

"2A. A printout of entry or a copy of printout referred to in sub-section (8) of section 2 shall be accompanied by the following, namely:

a) certificate to the effect that it is a printout of such entry or a copy of such printout by the principal accountant or branch manager; and

b) a certificate by a person in-charge of computer system containing a brief description of the computer system and the particulars of:

A) the safeguards adopted by the system to ensure that data is entered or any other operation performed only by authorised person;

B) the safeguards adopted to prevent and detect unauthorised change of data;

C) the safeguards available to retrieve data that is lost due to systemic failure or any other reasons;

D) the manner in which data is transferred from the system to removable media like floppies, discs, tapes or other electromagnetic data storage devices;

E) the mode of verification in order to ensure that data has been accurately transferred to such removable media;

F) the mode of identification of such data storage devices;

G) the arrangements for the storage and custody of such storage devices;

H) the safeguards to prevent and detect any tampering with the system; and

I) any other factor which will vouch for the integrity and accuracy of the system,

c) "a further certificate from the person in-charge of the computer system to the effect that to the best of his knowledge and belief, such computer system operated properly at the material time, he was provided with all the relevant data and the printout in question represents correctly, or is appropriately derived from, the relevant data,"

VI. RESERVE BANK OF INDIA ACT, 1934 (Amendment)

After the introduction of Information Technology Act 2000 and in absence of any provision relating to evidence it was necessary to amend the Reserve Bank of India Act, 1934 to deal with the offence relating to cyber crimes. In relation to cyber crime there are many sections which were substituted so some are newly inserted. The following sections are as follows:-

In the Reserve Bank of India Act there is only a single amendment has been made out i.e., under Section 58 as clause pp inserted after the introduction of Information Technology Act 2000.

Section 58- Power of Central Board to make Regulations

In this Section a new clause pp has been inserted after clause p as:-

"(pp) the regulation of fund transfer through electronic means between the banks or between the banks, and other financial institutions referred to in clause (c) of section 45-1, including the laying down of the conditions subject to which banks and other financial institutions shall participate in such fund transfers, the manner of such fund transfers and the right and obligations of the participants in such fund transfers.

VII- National Cyber Security Policy-2013

National Cyber Security Policy is a policy framework by Department of Electronics and Information Technology (DeitY)[1] It aims at protecting the public and private infrastructure from cyber attacks.[2] The policy also intends to safeguard "information, such as personal information (of web users), financial and banking information and sovereign data".

Vision

To build a secure and resilient cyberspace for citizens, business, and government and also to protect anyone from intervening in your privacy.

Mission

To protect information and information infrastructure in cyberspace, build capabilities to prevent and respond to cyber threat, reduce vulnerabilities and minimize damage from cyber incidents through a combination of institutional structures, people, processes, technology, and cooperation.

Objective

There are following objectives of National Cyber Security Policy 2013

i).To create a secure cyber ecosystem in the country, generate adequate trust and confidence in IT system and transactions in cyberspace and thereby enhance adoption of IT in all sectors of the economy.

ii).To create an assurance framework for the design of security policies and promotion and enabling actions for compliance to global security standards and best practices by way of conformity assessment (Product, process, technology & people).

iii).To strengthen the Regulatory Framework for ensuring a SECURE CYBERSPACE ECOSYSTEM.

iv).To enhance and create National and Sectoral level 24X7 mechanism for obtaining strategic information regarding threats to ICT infrastructure, creating scenarios for response, resolution and crisis management through effective predictive, preventive, protective response and recovery actions.

-To improve visibility of integrity of ICT products and services by establishing infrastructure for testing & validation of security of such product.

v).To create workforce for 500,000 professionals skilled in next 5 years through capacity building skill development and training.

vi).To provide fiscal benefit to businesses for adoption of standard security practices and processes.

vii).To enable Protection of information while in process, handling, storage & transit so as to safeguard privacy of citizen's data and reducing economic losses due to cyber crime or data theft.

viii).To enable effective prevention, investigation and prosecution of cyber crime and enhancement of law enforcement capabilities through appropriate legislative intervention.

Strategies

i).Creating a secured Ecosystem.

ii).Creating an assurance framework.

iii).Encouraging Open Standards.

iv).Strengthening The regulatory Framework.

v).Creating mechanism for Security Threats Early Warning, Vulnerability management and response to security threat.

vi).Securing E-Governance services.

vii).Protection and resilience of Critical Information Infrastructure.

viii).Promotion of Research and Development in cyber security.

ix).Reducing supply chain risks

x).Human Resource Development (fostering education and training programs) both in formal and informal sectors to support Nation's cyber security needs and build capacity.

xi).Creating cyber security awareness.

xii).Developing effective Public Private Partnership.

xiii).To develop bilateral and multilateral relationship in the area of cyber security with other country. (**Information sharing and cooperation**)

xiv).Prioritized approach for implementation.

Chapter Nine

Cyber Authorities in india

I- Certifying Authorities

As per Section 18 of The Information Technology Act, 2000 provides the required legal sanctity to the digital signatures based on asymmetric cryptosystems. The digital signatures are now accepted at par with handwritten signatures and the electronic documents that have been digitally signed are treated at par with paper documents.

The IT Act provides for the Controller of Certifying Authorities (CCA) to license and regulate the working of Certifying Authorities. The Certifying Authorities (CAs) issue digital signature certificates for electronic authentication of users.

The Controller of Certifying Authorities (CCA) has been appointed by the Central Government under section 17 of the Act for purposes of the IT Act. The Office of the CCA came into existence on November 1, 2000. It aims at promoting the growth of E-Commerce and E- Governance through the wide use of digital signatures.

The Controller of Certifying Authorities (CCA) has established the Root Certifying Authority (RCAI) of India under section 18(b) of the IT Act to digitally sign the public keys of Certifying Authorities (CA) in the country. The RCAI is operated as per the standards laid down under the Act.

The CCA certifies the public keys of CAs using its own private key, which enables users in the cyberspace to verify that a given certificate is issued by a licensed CA. For this purpose it operates, the Root Certifying Authority of India(RCAI). The CCA also maintains the Repository of Digital Certificates, which contains all the certificates issued to the CAs in the country.

II- Adjudicating Authorities

The Indian Information Technology Act, 2000 for the purpose of adjudging the commission of offence gives power to adjudication under this Act. Adjudication and Adjudication officer has been mentioned in sec 46 & 47 of IT Act:-

46. Power to adjudicate.–

(*1*) For the purpose of adjudging under this Chapter whether any person has committed a contravention of any of the provisions of this Act or of any rule, regulation, direction or order made there under which renders him liable to pay penalty or compensation, the Central Government shall, subject to the provisions of sub-section (*3*), appoint any officer not below the rank of a Director to the Government of India or an equivalent officer of a State Government to be an adjudicating officer for holding an inquiry in the manner prescribed by the Central Government.

(*1A*) The adjudicating officer appointed under sub-section (*1*) shall exercise jurisdiction to adjudicate matters in which the claim for injury or damage does not exceed rupees five crore:

Provided that the jurisdiction in respect of the claim for injury or damage exceeding rupees five crores shall vest with the competent court.

(*2*) The adjudicating officer shall, after giving the person referred to in sub section (*1*) a reasonable opportunity for making representation in the matter and if, on such inquiry, he is satisfied that the person has committed the contravention, he may impose such penalty or award such compensation as he thinks fit in accordance with the provisions of that section.

(*3*) No person shall be appointed as an adjudicating officer unless he possesses such experience in the field of Information Technology and legal or judicial experience as may be prescribed by the Central Government.

(*4*) Where more than one adjudicating officers are appointed, the Central Government shall specify by order the matters and places with respect to which such officers shall exercise their jurisdiction.

(*5*) Every adjudicating officer shall have the powers of a civil court which are conferred on the

(*a*) all proceedings before it shall be deemed to be judicial proceedings within the meaning of sections 193 and 228 of the Indian Penal Code (45 of 1860);

(*b*) shall be deemed to be a civil court for the purposes of sections 345 and 346 of the Code of Criminal Procedure, 1973 (2 of 1974);

(*c*) shall be deemed to be a civil court for purposes of Order XXI of the Civil Procedure Code, 1908 (5 of 1908).]

47. Factors to be taken into account by the adjudicating officer.–

While adjudging the quantum of compensation under this Chapter, the adjudicating officer shall have due regard to the following factors, namely:–

(*a*) the amount of gain of unfair advantage, wherever quantifiable, made as a result of the default;

(*b*) the amount of loss caused to any person as a result of the default;

(*c*) the repetitive nature of the default.

III- National Nodal Agency

Section 70 A of the IT Act deals with the provision of National Nodal Agency.

Section 70A of Information Technology Act states:

(1) The Central Government may, by notification published in the Official Gazette, designate any organisation of the Government as the national nodal agency in respect of Critical Information Infrastructure Protection.

(2) The national nodal agency designated under sub-section (1) shall be responsible for all measures including Research and Development relating to protection of Critical Information Infrastructure.

(3) The manner of performing functions and duties of the agency referred to in sub-section (1) shall be such as may be prescribed.

IV- Indian Computer Emergency Response Team

Section 70 B of the Information Technology prescribes about ICERT to serve as national agency for incident response:

(1) The Central Government shall, by notification in the Official Gazette, appoint an agency of the government to be called the Indian Computer Emergency Response Team.

(2) The Central Government shall provide the agency referred to in sub-section (1) with a Director General and such other officers and employees as may be prescribed.

(3) The salary and allowances and terms and conditions of the Director General and other officers and employees shall be such as may be prescribed.

(4) The Indian Computer Emergency Response Team shall serve as the national agency for performing the following functions in the area of Cyber Security,-

1. collection, analysis and dissemination of information on cyber incidents
2. forecast and alerts of cyber security incidents
3. emergency measures for handling cyber security incidents
4. coordination of cyber incidents response activities
5. issue guidelines, advisories, vulnerability notes and white papers relating to information security practices, procedures, prevention, response and reporting of cyber incidents
6. such other functions relating to cyber security as may be prescribed

2. (5) The manner of performing functions and duties of the agency referred to in sub-section (1) shall be such as may be prescribed.

6. (6) For carrying out the provisions of sub-section (4), the agency referred to in sub-section (1) may call for information and give direction to the service providers, intermediaries, data centers, body corporate and any other person

7. (7) Any service provider, intermediaries, data centers, body corporate or person who fails to provide the information called for or comply with the direction under sub-section (6), shall be punishable with imprisonment for a term which may extend to one year or with fine which may extend to one lakh rupees or with both.

8. (8) No Court shall take cognizance of any offence under this section, except on a complaint made by an officer authorized in this behalf by the agency referred to in sub-section (1).

V- Investigating Authority

The Information Technology Act empowers a Police officer not below the rank of Inspector for investigating any offence under this Act.

Further Section 80 of IT, Act presents the Power of police officer and other officers to enter, search, etc.-

(1) Notwithstanding anything contained in the Code of Criminal Procedure, 1973 (2 of 1974), any police officer, not below the rank of a Deputy Superintendent of Police, or any other officer of the Central Government or a State Government authorized by the Central Government in this behalf may enter any public place and search and arrest without warrant any person found therein who is reasonably suspected of having committed or of committing or of being about to commit any offence under this Act. Explanation.-For the purposes of this sub-section, the expression "public place" includes any public conveyance, any hotel, any shop or any other place intended for use by, or accessible to the public.

(2) Where any person is arrested under sub-section (1) by an officer other than a police officer, such officer shall, without unnecessary delay, take or send the person arrested before a magistrate having jurisdiction in the case or before the officer-in-charge of a police station.

(3) The provisions of the Code of Criminal Procedure, 1973 (2 of 1974), shall, subject to the provisions of this section, apply, so far as may be, in relation to any entry, search or arrest, made under this section.

VI - Cyber Regulations Advisory Committee

One of the brightest aspects of the ITA-2000 was the provision to have an apex advisory body called the Cyber Regulations Advisory Committee.

According to Section 88 of Information Technology Act, 2000 the Central Government shall, as soon as may be after the commencement of this Act, constitute a Committee called the "***Cyber Regulations Advisory*** Committee".

Sec 88 of Information Technology Act 2000 Stands as:-

Constitution of Advisory Committee:

(1) The Central Government shall, as soon as may be after the commencement of this Act, constitute a Committee called the Cyber Regulations Advisory Committee.

(2) The Cyber Regulations Advisory Committee shall consist of a Chairperson and such number of other official and non-official members representing the interests principally affected or having special knowledge of the subject-matter as the Central Government may deem fit.

(3) The Cyber Regulations Advisory Committee shall advise -

(a) the Central Government either generally as regards any rules or for any other purpose connected with this Act;

(b) the Controller in framing the regulations under this Act

The section captures an intention that the committee would consist of industry experts who are expected to guide the Government and the Controller regarding all aspects of the law. It is important to note that the section uses the words "representing the interests principally affected". This is a clear indication that the framers of the Act envisaged that there would be industry representation from those sections such as the IT industry, the Dot.Com industry, the Lawyer community etc.

Chapter Ten

Cyber Crime Status in india

The cyber crime status of India is very low in the world compared to other countries. The Internet Crime Report for 2019, released by USA's Internet Crime Complaint Centre (IC3) of the Federal Bureau of Investigation, has revealed that India stands third in the world among top 20 countries that are victims of internet crimes. As per the report, excluding the USA, the UK tops the list with 93,796 victims of internet crimes followed by Canada (3,721) and India (2,901).

cyber crimes in India from 2018-2020 almost doubled, according to statistics released by the National Crime Record Bureau (NCRB).

2019 - TOP 20 INTERNATIONAL VICTIM COUNTRIES

Excluding the United States[7]

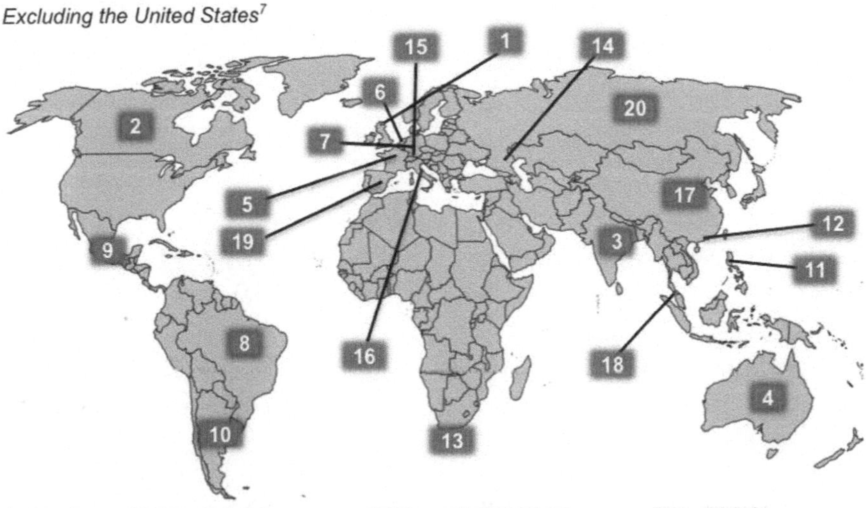

1. United Kingdom	93,796	6. Belgium	1,031	11. Philippines	561	16. Italy	428
2. Canada	3,721	7. Germany	850	12. Hong Kong	535	17. China	403
3. India	2,901	8. Brazil	628	13. South Africa	465	18. Malaysia	362
4. Australia	1,298	9. Mexico	605	14. Georgia	454	19. Spain	358
5. France	1,243	10. Argentina	578	15. Switzerland	438	20. Russian Federation	349

TABLE 9A.1

Cyber Crimes (State/UT-wise) - 2018-2020

SL	State/UT	2018	2019	2020	Mid-Year Projected Population (in Lakhs)	Rate of Total Cyber Crimes (2020)	Chargesheeting Rate (2020)
[1]	[2]	[3]	[4]	[5]	[6]	[7]	[8]
STATES:							
1	Andhra Pradesh	1207	1886	1899	526.0	3.6	40.1
2	Arunachal Pradesh	7	8	30	15.2	2.0	33.3
3	Assam	2022	2231	3530	347.9	10.1	19.4
4	Bihar	374	1050	1512	1219.0	1.2	65.0
5	Chhattisgarh	139	175	297	292.4	1.0	87.4
6	Goa	29	15	40	15.5	2.6	50.0
7	Gujarat	702	784	1283	691.7	1.9	47.1
8	Haryana	418	564	656	292.1	2.2	49.6
9	Himachal Pradesh	69	76	98	73.6	1.3	41.9
10	Jharkhand	930	1095	1204	381.2	3.2	53.0
11	Karnataka	5839	12020	10741	665.0	16.2	72.9
12	Kerala	340	307	426	353.7	1.2	70.6
13	Madhya Pradesh	740	602	699	837.6	0.8	85.6
14	Maharashtra	3511	4967	5496	1236.8	4.4	27.1
15	Manipur	29	4	79	31.4	2.5	0.0
16	Meghalaya	74	89	142	32.6	4.4	1.4
17	Mizoram	6	8	13	12.1	1.1	57.1
18	Nagaland	2	2	8	21.8	0.4	-
19	Odisha	843	1485	1931	454.7	4.2	33.5
20	Punjab	239	243	378	301.8	1.3	62.4
21	Rajasthan	1104	1762	1354	786.1	1.7	26.8
22	Sikkim	1	2	0	6.7	0.0	-
23	Tamil Nadu	295	385	782	761.7	1.0	53.1
24	Telangana	1205	2691	5024	375.4	13.4	42.5
25	Tripura	20	20	34	40.4	0.8	26.3
26	Uttar Pradesh	6280	11416	11097	2289.3	4.8	49.9
27	Uttarakhand	171	100	243	113.1	2.1	63.0
28	West Bengal	335	524	712	977.2	0.7	45.9
	TOTAL STATE(S)	**26931**	**44511**	**49708**	**13151.8**	**3.8**	**47.5**
UNION TERRITORIES :							
29	A&N Islands	7	2	5	4.0	1.3	62.5
30	Chandigarh	30	23	17	12.0	1.4	30.0
31	D&N Haveli and Daman & Diu[@]	0[+]	3[+]	3	10.4	0.3	100.0
32	Delhi	189	115	168	203.2	0.8	66.3
33	Jammu & Kashmir[@]	73[*]	73[*]	120	133.4	0.9	42.4
34	Ladakh[@]	-	-	1	3.0	0.3	-
35	Lakshadweep	4	4	3	0.7	4.4	-
36	Puducherry	14	4	10	15.5	0.6	100.0
	TOTAL UT(S)	**317**	**224**	**327**	**382.1**	**0.9**	**59.7**
	TOTAL ALL INDIA	**27248**	**44735**	**50035**	**13533.9**	**3.7**	**47.5**

- Crime Rate is calculated as Crime Incidence per one lakh of population

TABLE 9A.1 Page 1 of 1

- Population Source: Report of Technical group on Population Projections(July, 2020) National Commission on Population, MoHFW
- As per data provided by States/UTs • States/UTs may not be compared purely on the basis of crime figures

'+' Combined data of erstwhile D&N Haveli UT and Daman & Diu UT

'*' Data of erstwhile Jammu & Kashmir State including Ladakh

'@' Data of newly created Union Territory

TABLE 9A.5

Police Disposal of Cyber Crime Cases (State/UT-wise) - 2020 (Concluded)

SL	State/UT	Total Cases Disposed Off by Police (Col. 7+8+15+18)	Cases Quashed at Investigation Stage	Cases Stayed at Investigation Stage	Cases Pending Invsgn. at end of the year (Cols. 6-9-19-20)	Charge sheeting Rate (Col.18/19*100)	Pendency Percentage (Col.22/6*100)
[1]	[2]	[19]	[20]	[21]	[22]	[23]	[24]
STATES:							
1	Andhra Pradesh	784	0	0	3689	40.1	82.5
2	Arunachal Pradesh	3	0	0	41	33.3	93.2
3	Assam	1983	0	0	4848	19.4	71.0
4	Bihar	1001	0	0	1694	65.0	62.9
5	Chhattisgarh	174	0	0	287	87.4	62.3
6	Goa	12	0	0	50	50.0	80.6
7	Gujarat	1009	4	3	466	47.1	31.5
8	Haryana	446	0	0	558	49.6	55.6
9	Himachal Pradesh	74	0	0	91	41.9	55.2
10	Jharkhand	872	0	2	2295	53.0	72.5
11	Karnataka	3901	0	1	26248	72.9	87.1
12	Kerala	228	3	1	620	70.6	72.9
13	Madhya Pradesh	520	1	0	677	85.6	56.1
14	Maharashtra	3329	3	0	10669	27.1	76.2
15	Manipur	1	0	0	201	0.0	99.5
16	Meghalaya	74	0	0	194	1.4	72.4
17	Mizoram	14	0	0	8	57.1	36.4
18	Nagaland	0	0	0	10	-	100.0
19	Odisha	843	0	0	3600	33.5	81.0
20	Punjab	170	1	0	659	62.4	79.4
21	Rajasthan	1270	0	0	713	26.8	36.0
22	Sikkim	0	0	0	2	-	100.0
23	Tamil Nadu	254	2	0	1248	53.1	83.0
24	Telangana	2209	0	0	5664	42.5	71.9
25	Tripura	19	0	0	51	26.3	72.9
26	Uttar Pradesh	10001	0	0	6833	49.9	40.6
27	Uttarakhand	92	0	0	285	63.0	75.6
28	West Bengal	388	3	0	1345	45.9	77.5
	TOTAL STATE(S)	**29671**	**17**	**7**	**73046**	**47.5**	**71.1**
UNION TERRITORIES:							
29	A&N Islands	8	0	0	7	62.5	46.7
30	Chandigarh	10	0	0	68	30.0	87.2
31	D&N Haveli and Daman & Diu	1	0	0	6	100.0	85.7
32	Delhi	92	0	0	718	66.3	88.6
33	Jammu & Kashmir	33	0	0	261	42.4	88.8
34	Ladakh	0	0	0	2	-	100.0
35	Lakshadweep	0	0	0	11	-	100.0
36	Puducherry	5	0	0	23	100.0	82.1
	TOTAL UT(S)	**149**	**0**	**0**	**1096**	**59.7**	**88.0**
	TOTAL ALL INDIA	**29820**	**17**	**7**	**74142**	**47.5**	**71.3**

• As per data provided by States/UTs

•States/UTs may not be compared purely on the basis of crime figures

TABLE 9A.5 Page 4 of 4

That in 2020 Pendency rate of disposal of cyber crime related complaints by police is 71.3% which is very low but the crime rate is increasing day by day.

TABLE 9A.7

Court Disposal of Cyber Crime Cases (State/UT-wise) - 2020 (Concluded)

SL	State/UT	Cases which Trials were Completed (Col.15+Col.16+ Col.17)	Cases Disposed off by Courts (Col.11+Col.18)	Cases Pending Trial at End of the Year (Col.5-Col.19)	Conviction Rate (Col.15/ Col.18)*100	Pendency Percentage (Col.20/ Col.5)*100
[1]	[2]	[18]	[19]	[20]	[21]	[22]
STATES:						
1	Andhra Pradesh	104	150	994	5.8	86.9
2	Arunachal Pradesh	0	0	5	-	100.0
3	Assam	41	43	1115	0.0	96.3
4	Bihar	0	0	1500	-	100.0
5	Chhattisgarh	10	15	440	30.0	96.7
6	Goa	1	1	49	0.0	98.0
7	Gujarat	4	4	1766	0.0	99.8
8	Haryana	9	11	813	0.0	98.7
9	Himachal Pradesh	1	1	174	0.0	99.4
10	Jharkhand	171	171	961	73.1	84.9
11	Karnataka	21	2583	1040	9.5	28.7
12	Kerala	7	8	1026	0.0	99.2
13	Madhya Pradesh	49	56	2062	28.6	97.4
14	Maharashtra	37	44	5168	8.1	99.2
15	Manipur	0	0	7	-	100.0
16	Meghalaya	0	0	35	-	100.0
17	Mizoram	2	2	16	100.0	88.9
18	Nagaland	0	0	1	-	100.0
19	Odisha	1	1	1049	0.0	99.9
20	Punjab	6	7	304	16.7	97.7
21	Rajasthan	50	57	1418	48.0	96.1
22	Sikkim	1	1	0	0.0	0.0
23	Tamil Nadu	39	39	504	17.9	92.8
24	Telangana	336	481	1454	83.3	75.1
25	Tripura	0	0	14	-	100.0
26	Uttar Pradesh	725	733	12851	88.6	94.6
27	Uttarakhand	1	1	239	0.0	99.6
28	West Bengal	6	6	758	0.0	99.2
	TOTAL STATE(S)	**1622**	**4415**	**35763**	**68.4**	**89.0**
UNION TERRITORIES:						
29	A&N Islands	0	0	19	-	100.0
30	Chandigarh	3	4	35	33.3	89.7
31	D&N Haveli and Daman & Diu	0	0	7	-	100.0
32	Delhi	0	0	316	-	100.0
33	Jammu & Kashmir	1	1	81	0.0	98.8
34	Ladakh	0	0	1	-	100.0
35	Lakshadweep	0	0	0	-	-
36	Puducherry	0	0	14	-	100.0
	TOTAL UT(S)	**4**	**5**	**473**	**25.0**	**99.0**
	TOTAL ALL INDIA	**1626**	**4420**	**36236**	**68.3**	**89.1**

• As per data provided by States/UTs

• States/UTs may not be compared purely on the basis of crime figures

TABLE 9A.7 Page 4 of 4

That in 2020 the pendency rate of disposal of cyber crime related cases in the court is 89.1% which is approximately none.

The reasons of the increasing of cyber cases and such a low pendency rate of disposal of complaints by the police and the disposal of the cases by the Courts are as follows:-

A Lacuna In The Information Technology Act

Despite the various advantages Indian Information Technology has following flaws:

(1) Jurisdiction: Information Technology Act does not cover the important issue of the jurisdiction which is very important legal aspect in deciding the place of filing the case because cyber crime is the only crime which doesn't needs the physical presence where the crime has been committing or committed. In cyberspace one can commit crime from other place or state or country resultantly it can't be decided under which jurisdiction the case will be registered or who will investigate the case.

(2) Electronic Records: Whether the amendments has been made regarding electronic records but still in the Information technology act it has not been clarifies that what electronic records which are digitally signed will be accepted as evidence and how the evidence will be produced and what are the process to check the authenticity of that electronic record the most common type of example of this is E-mail which is a very common kind of communication through internet.

(3) Intellectual Property Rights: That even after of section 81 which is incorporated by the Information Technology (Amendment) Act, 2008 which provides that this Act shall not restrict any person from exercising any right conferred under the copyright Act, 1957 or the Patent Act, 1970 but still does not contain any special provisions which safeguards the intellectual property rights such as copyrights, trademarks, or patents etc. Today, IPRs in digital medium is an important issue especially copyright issues, trademark issues and patent issues in digital medium which remain neither described nor penalised by Information Technology Act, 2000 specifically.

(4) Domain Names Infringement: E-commerce is mainly based upon domain name instead of that Information Technology Act neither includes Domain names infringement, cyber squatting, typo squatting, spamming nor such offence has been penalized under the act.

(5) Only broad kind of Cyber crimes and contraventions are covered: The Information Technology Act, 2000 covers only common kind of Cyber crimes and contraventions which are caused frequently. There were only 10 offences initially under IT Act, 2000 but as the use of technology has been increased by the criminals it becomes necessary to increase to add more cyber offences under the Act. Resultantly 13 new cyber offences were inserted whereas seven existing offences were substituted in the information Technology (Amendment) Act, 2008. It is important to note that various crimes like cyber stalking, violating privacy of a person, cyber terrorism, receiving and retaining stolen computer resource and offences against computer are made punishable by the information Technology (Amendment) Act, 2008. Further, Using communication device for committing any offence is also punishable. However, following loopholes regarding cyber offences are still there:

(a) The term cyber crime and cyber offence as such is not defined under Information Technology Act, 2000.

(b) Offences mentioned under Chapter 11 are not exhaustive.

(c) No illustration or examples of such offences are given.

(d) Some offences like chat room abuses, watching porn websites, domain name infringement, spamming, cyber squatting, data diddling etc. are still not covered.

(6) Lack of International Cooperation: Due to absence of any treaty signed by India relating to cyber crime there is lack of international cooperation, cyber crimes cannot be handled by isolated national efforts.

(7) Important documents such as power of attorney, etc. not covered: Another loophole of Act, 2000 is that it is not applicable to various documents covered under Schedule I. However important documents such as power of attorney, will trust, any contract for sale of immovable property and a negotiable instrument are mentioned under schedule I hence, not covered under IT Act, 2000. Therefore where E-contract relating to immovable property is formed or will is made in electronic form then Information Technology Acct shall not be applicable.

(8) No parameter for Implementation: This Act does not lay down the parameters for its implementation. In India, government and police officials are not computer or technology expert. Even judges are not fully sensitized to technology. Therefore, question of implementation of Information Technology Act, 2000 does not arise.

Therefore, for the proper implementation of this Act there must be sensitization of judiciary, police official to the technology.

B- Lack of Awareness in Public

That whether the users of smart phones and internet are increasing day by day but still many people are not aware about "What is Cyber Crime?" and "How it happens?" and it happening in the rural as well as urban areas. The proof that there are lots of victims of a common type of cyber crime i.e., ATM Fraud, OTP Fraud, Banking Fraud etc. which is happened with many people daily in which some are reported whereas many are hidden due to lack of knowledge of taking action on such victimised. That instead of that due to lack of awareness in the public regarding cyber crime the people are being victims of cyber crime. That if the people are get aware about the way of committing crime the cyber crime rate will fall down speadily but the vice versa is happening.

C- Greed

That in India earning of money easily and become rich instantly is as common as every 2nd people thing like that and the criminals taking benefit of that and due to this greed people are easily victimised of a Cyber Crime. Cyber criminals are as expert that they observe that greed in the voice of the victim and taking benefit of that they attack on the victim again and again until the victim realized that he became a victim of Cyber Crime.

Chapter Eleven

Prevention & Suggestions

I. Preventive of Cyber Crime

Despite penal provisions and preventive measures provided in the Indian Penal Code and the I.T. Act, a perusal of cyber crime statistics of preceding years clearly indicates that there has been no decline in the crime rate and on the contrary, they are recording a steady rising trend. There are many new cyber crimes emerging which need improvised investigative and legal techniques and skills to handle them efficiently. **Prevention is always better than cure.** It is always better to take certain precautions while operating the net. Anybody should make them his part of cyber life.

The process of crime prevention essentially requires cooperation and active support of citizens, institution, industries and the Government alike. Therefore, a sound strategy for prevention of Cyber crime necessitates mobilisation of community participation in combating this menace. This calls for participative role of all those who perceive that the growing incidence of Cyber crime is a potential danger to society as a whole. It also calls for self protection initiatives by the people who are vulnerable to Cyber crimes. They must have adequate knowledge and awareness about the nature and gravity of these crimes and the dangers fraught by them.

There are following preventive measures which can safe from cyber crime:-

i. To prevent cyber stalking avoid disclosing any information pertaining to one self.

ii. Always avoid sending any photograph online particularly to strangers and chat friends as there have been incidents of misuse of the photographs.

iii. Always use latest and update antivirus software to guard against virus attacks.

iv. Always keep back up volumes so that one may not suffer data loss in case of virus contamination

v. Never send your credit card number to any site that is not secured, to guard against frauds.

vi. Always keep a watch on the sites that your children are accessing to prevent any kind of harassment or depravation in children. .

vii. Use of firewalls may be beneficial.

viii. Develop a communication with the childrens especially in case of difference in their behaviors.

ix.Do not overuse or addict of social media.

x.Never believe and transmit any social media news without verifying the same.

II. Suggestions

In view of the expanding dimensions of computer-related crimes, there is need for adopting appropriate regulatory legal measures and gearing up the law enforcement mechanism to tackle the problem of Cyber crime with stern hands. Even a short delay in investigation may allow cyber criminals enough time to delete or erase the important data to evade detection, which may cause huge loss to the internet user or the victim.

i). Special Statute:-

Special Statutes on cyber crime is required to be passed to deal with the new form of crimes and to protect digital data. It will include:-

a). Law for Saftey of Banking

Internet Banking involves not just the banks and their customers, but numerous third parties too. Information held by banks about their customers, their transactions etc. changes hand several times. It is impossible for the banks to retain information within their own computer networks.

Internet Banking involves not just the banks and their customers, but numerous third parties too. Information held by banks about their customers, their transactions etc. changes hand several times. It is impossible for the banks to retain information within their own computer networks. A statute addressing various issues related to privacy is of utmost importance today, if not an entire act can be brought into force, then at least specific provisions relating to privacy and data protection be incorporated into the Act.

b). Privacy Protection

Privacy and data protection are important issues that need to be addressed today as information technology assumes greater importance in personal, professional and commercial spheres. The European Union and the United States have strict policies relating to privacy and protection of personal data when such data or information is being transferred out of their domain.

c). Cyber War

The issue of Cyber War has also not been discussed in the Act. International law is an important part of any legal regime and due provisions need to be made in congruence with the international framework of laws. India, in recent times, has faced a number of cyber attacks from China and the Chinese hackers have overridden the Firewalls on Indian databases like a Mongol army on the rampage. In the 26/11 attacks, a number of classified data were provided as intel to the perpetrators from neighboring nations conspiring against India. There are no provisions in the Act to make such perpetrators liable for their actions.